THE BRITISH EMPIRE

ITS ORIGIN AND DESTINY

—BY—

EDWARD BYERS

OTTAWA

———————

———————

OTTAWA
James T. Pattison, Printer and Publisher, 370 Bank St., Ottawa
1921.

FOREWORD.

The allusions to "articles" in these pages arise from the fact that the first eighteen chapters are a reprint of articles written for "The Sentinel," Toronto. The publication in book form was urgently requested by more than a hundred readers, in kind letters of appreciation from all parts of Canada, and from several in the U.S.A. There was some opposition also; discouraging at first, but—"Sweet are the uses of adversity"—I am thereby enabled to give both sides in one volume; leaving my readers to take their choice.

It will be noted that, towards the end, the story devolves, more or less, into an account of the life and adventures of Jeremiah the prophet. The reason for this is that I found much difficulty in following the thread of these "adventures" myself, so I resolved to tackle it and elucidate it as far as possible, within the limits of my space; with the result that I have now a much clearer idea of this most important part of our study than when I set out. I trust this will be the experience of the reader.

E. B.

Ottawa, Nov. 30, 1921.

The British Empire

ITS ORIGIN AND DESTINY.

CHAPTER I.

INTRODUCTORY NOTES.

There exists in many minds, here in Canada as in other parts of the Empire, a strange antipathy to the term "Imperialism;" and this antipathy is by no means confined to those who are manifestly disloyal to the British connection. Even amongst loyal Canadians there is a widespread reluctance to accept the designation of "Imperialists." Many who would readily subscribe to the sentiment "Canada for the Canadians," without meaning thereby republicanism or separation from the Empire, are less enthusiastic about such an Imperial motto as "The Empire First"— "Canada for the Empire." They draw the line at "Imperialism." Yet no one who will intelligently study the constitution of our Empire can dispute the fact that British imperialism is the truest form of nationalism. Each nation of the Empire to-day owes its national existence to the imperialism of the British Empire. Therein lies its security as a nation. This statement can be proven in short order. For instance, if there were no imperialism there would be no British Empire. If there were no British Empire there would, of course, be no British navy; and if there were no British navy, Canada would at this moment be under the yoke of Germany, instead of being the free, unhampered whether they will it or not, to be the means whereby God's purpose shall be fulfilled. When—"the nations shall know that I am the Lord." "This people have I formed for myself; they shall show forth My praise." (Isaiah 43:21).

To recall the heading of this article—"The Origin of the British Empire"—How far back shall we go for that ? "Julius Caesar, having completed the conquest of Gaul, cast his eyes upon Britain." That was the way our school histories started out to tell Britain's history   Julius Caesar was only an episode in the history of Britain. For the origin of Britain, the covenant land, we must go back to the time of the covenant, centuries before Julius Caesar or the Roman Empire were heard of. We read that Abram came out of Ur of the Chaldees, and dwelt for a time in Haran; and in Genesis 12:1, "Now the Lord said unto Abram, Get thee out of thy country, and from thy kindred, and from thy father's house, unto a land that I will show thee." We may, perhaps, take that as the beginning. But what has it all to do with the British ? Just this. God Almighty then and there made a covenant, an **everlasting** covenant, with His servant Abram, to give to him and to his seed certain temporal birthright blessings; the possession of which blessings identify the British people as the seed of Abraham. The object of God's giving these blessings to a certain chosen people is very plainly portrayed in the Scripture—it is, in short, that they, of all others, should be his servants in extending blessings to all the nations of the earth. (See Gen. 12:2) "I will make of thee a great nation, and I will bless thee, and make thy name great, and thou shalt be a blessing." There was God's purpose. His chosen people, the seed of Abraham, were chosen for service. Evidence of this purpose is traceable all through the text of the promises. Read your Bible and see if this is not clear. Of the seed of Abraham should come the Saviour of the world and the Redeemer of Israel. By the seed of Abraham should the Gospel of the Saviour be spread that all nations might be blest. The terms of the Abrahamic covenant are quite definite. The maker of the covenant is God, and therefore, the covenant is everlasting and unalterable—Read and see. Gen. 17:7-19, "Thou shalt call his name Isaac; and I will establish my covenant with him for an everlasting covenant, and with his seed after him."

The covenant was renewed and reiterated over and over again, to Jacob, to Joseph, to David; if anything in the Bible is clear, this one thing is clear—that the covenant of God with His chosen people is immutable and unchangeable. No provisos whatever are put in, and no subsequent sin and disobedience on the part of the seed of Abraham could foil the unalterable purpose of God. The promises, in short, were not made to one people only to be "fulfilled" to someone else. The breaking by the children of Israel of the Mosaic covenant or law, which came four hundred and thirty years later, could not, as Saint Paul tells us, annul the promise.

The blessings that might have followed obedience to the law were conditional on that obedience, and they were foredoomed to failure of realization. But the promises are based on the unconditional covenant of grace. Nor was the covenant at all changed by the coming of Christ, by which so many good people suppose or assume the whole venue to be altered, so that now any and every Christian believer, of no matter what race, becomes an inheritor of the special blessings allotted by God's covenant to one race of people, and to no other.

Here is perhaps the greatest contradiction in the conclusions of accepted theology—that the precious death and atonement of God the Son should nullify and make void the promises of God the Father. Now that, absurd as it seems, is the logical or rather illogical conclusion to which

the teaching of many, nay, the great majority, of our
Christian expositors and teachers tends. Who is not familiar with the glib statement that because of the sin of the
Children of Israel they were cast off and all the blessings
that might have been theirs went to the Gentiles ! In that
case what becomes of the everlastingness of the covenant ?
Christ Himself told the Jews that the kingdom was to be
taken from them and given to a nation bringing forth the
fruits thereof. Was He forgetting God's everlasting covenant ? Most certainly not.

I do not need any training in college theology to convince
me that the "nation" to which the kingdom was to be
given must necessarily be also of the seed of Abraham, else
would all the promises be broken. Did not the seed of
Abraham, which inherited the promises, consist of the
Twelve Tribes of Israel ? Is it not true that it was only
the House of Judah or the Jews to whom our Lord was
speaking, and from whom He said the kingdom was to be
taken ?

So far from the promises being nullified by the coming
of Christ, it is by Him they are confirmed. (Romans 15:8).
It is He who has redeemed the chosen people of the Father
back into their inheritance. Both Houses of Israel were disobedient to the law. Both Houses had been visited with
dire punishment long prior to the advent of Christ. One
House has accepted the Redeemer, and are being blest, and
used, according to the promises. The other House, the
Jews, still reject their Redeemer, and are, therefore, not yet
redeemed or brought back; they are still of necessity under
the curse of the broken law.

But, again, what has all this to do with the British ?
Let us see. Amongst the temporal blessings promised by
God to Abraham was the possession of certain land. Genesis
13: 14, 15. "And the Lord said unto Abram—Lift up
now thine eyes and look from the place where thou art,

northward, and southward, and eastward, and westward. For all the land which thou seest, to thee will I give it, and to thy seed forever." The land in which Abraham stood was Mesopotamia. All around him was the "Promised Land," extending from Lebanon on the north, to the river of Egypt on the south; from the Mediterranean on the west, to the Euphrates on the east. Palestine itself is but a fraction of the land of the covenant. The Jews never possessed this land, but only a small portion of it, known as Judea. What has become of God's covenant? The land which God promised to the seed of Abraham for ever is in the possession of the British; some of it has been in their possession for years; some of it He has given them for a certain purpose in this year 1920. God promised it to the seed of Abraham for ever, and He has given it to the British. What does it mean? Why it can only mean that the British people are the seed of Abraham; and the covenant land has come into the possession of the "Covenant-People"—the "Brit-ish" in fulfilment of the promise of God made to our forefathers.

Let atheists say that our God is a breaker of covenants; but Christians surely cannot join the atheists in that assertion. On the covenants of God then is based the belief that the British people are the seed of Abraham of the Ten-tribed House of Israel. This is the real foundation of the British Empire. Laugh it to scorn who will, but in doing so they must dishonor the Author of the covenant; for when God Almighty makes covenants and promises they are not scraps of paper. They must come to their ultimate fulfilment, and they must be fulfilled to the last letter.

Let us, then, as Canadians, cherish our birthright as Britishers and Anglo-Saxons. Let us leave scoffing at British imperialism to such modern Esaus as Lindsay Crawford and his puny ilk. We, who have another faith, will not despise our birthright.

CHAPTER II.

In our second article on this subject we will, for the present, assume that there is no dispute as to the premise already laid down—that the covenant promises of God are destined to be fulfilled; albeit this assumption, reasonable and fundamental as it seems, is unfortunately not borne out by fact. True, there are very few who will not admit in the abstract that all God's promises must be fulfilled; yet there is a majority who contradict themselves by telling us that such and such a passage of Scripture is "not to be taken literally," which means the virtual cancellation of the passages as far as their philosophy is concerned, though the very passages which they thus discredit have very little sense or meaning, not to say apparent truth, apart from the literal. We shall go into this later on, but for the moment will assume that the point is conceded. We have also seen that the covenant promises were of grace—unconditional. Had they been conditional on man's faithfulness and sinlessness they would not be worthy of discussion now—a useless record of things which might have been—gone by default ages ago.

Nor were they mere promises of blessing to a favoured and chosen race. Far more: they were statements of God's will and determination to use the race so chosen in accomplishment of His purpose towards all mankind. "All the nations of the earth" were to be influenced by this people, whoever they were and are. Can you call to mind a people whose sphere of influence extends to all the nations of the earth? More anon. The fact of being chosen to serve was the greatest blessing of all, though it imposed the white man's burden of responsibility on the shoulders of the chosen servants. The promises then, being unconditional, did not depend on the faithfulness of the seed of Abraham, but on the faithfulness of the God of Abraham. A sure foundation!

Well indeed might it have been had the chosen people been faithful and obedient. But God was under no illusions —"I knew thou would'st deal very treacherously, and wast called a transgressor from the womb"; "O that thou hadst hearkened to my commandments! then had thy peace been as a river, and thy righteousness as the waves of the sea." (Isaiah 48:8-18). Here is a humbling thought. We have been blaming the ex-Kaiser for the late war. Well, here is where God lays the blame. David also, the servant of God, was doomed to make war all his days. In the history of Britain, as we know it, it has been the same. Mr. Gladstone once remarked, in a speech delivered at a time when the world was a heaven of peace compared to the present: "It is a horrible fact that somewhere or other, in one corner of the earth or another, we are always at war." Yet all the time our peace might have been as a river. When we boast, let us boast of the good hand of God which has kept us to this day. But, despite their sins, God was bound by a covenant to use this people, and no other. He was also bound by His own character of justice to punish them for their sins—"For Mine own sake, even for Mine own sake, will I do it: for how should My name be polluted? and I will not give My glory to another." The chosen race, then, had to work out their appointed destiny under the sore handicap of their own sins.

Perhaps it is getting ahead of the argument, but one feels prompted at this point to remark that a certain destiny seems always to have been existent in the conscience of the Anglo-Saxon people from the earliest recorded time. Despite the "Weird," or death-goddess of our forefathers, duties had to be performed. In the song of Beowulf in his last fight he cries; "To us it shall be as our Weird betides; that Weird that is every man's lord"; "Go the Weird as it will, each man of us shall abide the end of his life work; let him that may work, work his doomed deeds ere death come !" Shirking of responsibility cannot be numbered as one of the bad traits of the Anglo-Saxon character. We have our faults, but not that one, as witness all the world ! Alike in the legendary times of Woden-worship, the romantic and chivalrous times of Richard Coeur-de-Lion, the brave days of Pitt, down to the no less brave, but far more brutally prosaic days of Lloyd George, the Anglo-Saxon has answered the compelling call to "work his doomed deeds." Other nations may pride themselves on their astuteness in keeping out of trouble, but John Bull has drifted into the position of a sort of world's policeman. Not of intent, or by set purpose. It has all come about in what is regarded as the natural course of events, and hardly anybody stops to ask why.

The "why" of it is a mystery which may in some measure be solved by a study of the blessings promised forever to "a great nation" forecast in the Scriptures, and by a comparison of these with the blessings, marks and identification signs which pertain to a great nation, and, necessarily, only to one great nation now existent. The full solution of the mystery is, of course, bound up in the future and as independent prophecy does not come within the scope or the gift of the present writer, we are taking things as we find them. That word "forever" clinches the fact that the nation referred to must be in existence now, in our own times, and the question naturally arising is: Which of the nations is it ?

The blessings were to descend through Isaac. "In Isaac shall thy seed be called." We are told that the Anglo-Saxons took the latter part of their name from Saxony, in Germany, but there are others (the writer amongst the number) who believe that the Saxons, on the contrary, gave their name to that section of country in which in the course of their wanderings as outcast Israelites they settled for a time. Is it any more unreasonable to conclude that Saxony took its name from the Saxons, than that England took its name from the Angles ?

In a book entitled "British-Israel Truth" (edited by the late Ven. Archdeacon Denis Hanan, M.A., D.D., and H. Aldersmith, M.B., F.R.C.S.) to which the writer is indebted for a good deal of information, comparison is made as follows: "Saak is the root word of I-saac, meaning 'laughter.' . . . . The Saka of the Monuments; the Sakai or Sacæ of the Greek and Roman geographers; Saxe, Sach-sen, Saxon, are all reasonable derivations of the root." It will be noted that there is no positive or dogmatic assertion here; but I submit, if this definition be true, then there does exist a "great nation," called in the name of Isaac—Saxons, or Isaac's-sons. Otherwise, if it be not true, there is no such nation or race on earth that can be said to be "called in the name of Isaac." On the latter point, at any rate, one can be quite dogmatic and positive. We are only inquirers, Do you know of any other such nation ? A hole-and-corner nation will not do. It is of no use to "discover" such a race, as some people profess to do, hidden away in the Himalayan Mountains, or in Tibet; no, nor the Gypsies ! It must not only be a great nation, but the greatest on earth; and as we know positively that the greatest race on earth is the Anglo-Saxon, we are satisfied in our discovery of the nation prophesied. We have assumed that the promises must be fulfilled, and in any case there seems no good reason for supposing that this one is "not to be taken literally," so we include it in the number of our identification marks.

Again, when Abraham had proved his willingness to sacrifice the son of his hopes, further blessings were heaped upon him, "In blessing I will bless thee, and in multiplying I will multiply thy seed as the stars of the heaven, and as the sand which is upon the seashore" (Figurative language, no doubt, but literal in the sense of its application), "and thy seed shall possess the gate of his enemies." (Gen. 22: 17). This latter promise naturally had a special attraction and significance to such a strategist as the late Admiral Sir John Fisher, a British Israelite, it seems, by conviction. Admiral Fisher points out that the five sea gates of the world are now in the possession of the British, viz., the Straits of Dover, the Strait of Gibraltar, the Suez Canal, the Straits of Malacca, and the Cape of Good Hope. And the late Admiral's conclusion is a question: "Are we not the lost tribes ?" Personally I should say we are found. Should anyone raise objection to the omission of the Panama Canal, I answer— that "gate" is also in the possession of a branch of the Anglo-Saxon race; of the tribe of Manasseh, it is believed; and in any case, thank God, it is not a "gate of our enemies"; it is held by friends! Oh, we have enemies down there, but not among the Anglo-Saxons. If the Admiral were living now he might add to his list, the Dardanelles, the Kiel Canal, the Cattegat, etc. And we did not go to war in order to get these passages. What does it mean ? Details necessary to a wonderful destiny ?

CHAPTER III.

Before going on to consider the peculiar significance of the language used in God's promises to Jacob, we must dwell briefly on the promises to Isaac. It will not be possible to take more than a cursory glance at any of these grand passages, on which volumes of sermons have been preached, while congregations of Britishers languished in the pews, because—it had all happened so long ago, and they had heard it so often—without ever being told that it meant any more to them as a race than to the Zulus.

I once heard a Canadian lady lecturer remark that she wanted to hear sermons that dealt with ourselves, and with the problems of our own times. She didn't believe so much thought should be spent on "Moses in the bulrushes." She had nothing against Moses, but she liked Abraham Lincoln as well. She wanted to hear about real live people, for "there wasn't any particular virtue attaching to a man because he was a few thousand years dead." The lady was quite logical in what she meant to convey; she wasn't disparaging religion at all; but in one of her later remarks she showed what was the matter with her—She was too broad-minded. She "didn't see why we should regard ourselves as superior to other nations just because we were British, or because we were Anglo-Saxons." That was just it. She "did not see." And she was only one of the victims of the "blindness in part which has happened to Israel, until the fulness of the Gentiles be come in." Rom. 11:25.

Nor should we claim any virtue to ourselves because we are Anglo-Saxons; but it is the glorious heritage which has descended to us down through the ages. Shall we esteem it lightly? Dare we under-value an inheritance so important as to call forth the confirmatory oath of the Almighty ?

We find God speaking to Isaac, in Gen. 26. "Sojourn in this land, and I will be with thee, and will bless thee, for unto thee, and unto thy seed, I will give all these countries, and I will perform the oath which I sware unto Abraham thy father." "And," twice it is repeated, "I will give unto thy seed all these countries." (Countries over which the British flag now flies). "Because that Abraham obeyed my voice, and kept my charge, my commandments, my statutes and my laws." Note the "Because." What a hollow promise it would have been had He said, "If thy seed keep my commandments, my statutes and my laws." God had exacted a most terrible proof of the faith of Abraham; but for our familiarity with the story it would appal the imagination. The knife was drawn and the father's hand was raised over his son; the supreme deed of faith was actually performed in the heart of Abraham. Having proved the worthiness of this man to be the progenitor of a race which God had planned on setting apart for the blessing of all nations, how could He mock the man who had come through such an ordeal, by making promises, the fulfilment of which depended on the faithfulness of generations yet unborn ? God did not mock Abraham with any such promise as that. But, the objector will ask, how could a just God grant all these promised blessings to a people who were to be sinful, faithless, and disobedient ? Yes, He can; and He vindicates His justice in that "Because." He was to punish the disobedient Israelites; but obviously not by breaking His oath to Abraham. Nothing can prevent the fulfilment of that oath, nor delay the time pre-arranged for the denouement of God's plans.

A great truth will begin to dawn on us when we realize that the plans made under oath by the Supreme Being, are being fulfilled in and by the instrumentality of our own race—the great truth that the Supreme Being has made provision for His creation throughout all ages. His greatest creation, the part made in His own image, had fallen by sin, and was to bring upon itself dire times and awful problems, under which it was to groan, as it does at this day; and the Creator, foreseeing it all, has pledged Himself, by His most holy oath, that He has made provision for its deliverance, both temporal and eternal. We must not be misunderstood as placing temporal blessings before the spiritual nor on an equality; but we must insist that promises of lands and territory and multitudinous seed, and great nationhood, are promises pertaining to the temporal, and are the great marks of our identity. They are the proofs that God's plan embraces care for the problems and perplexities of our own times.

I am not a pessimist, but I have not much use for the preacher whose theme is "Cheer up, the world is not so bad after all." That line of preaching would not help a toothache. I am not a pessimist when I remember that these dark and troublous times of ours were all foreseen by God, and have been provided for; and that is the only intelligent ground any man in these days can have for his optimism. Nor have I much use for the "dire foreboders," who limit themselves to the exhortation to "Flee from the wrath to come"; as if it were all up with us in this world. Why, we are not to "flee" in that sense at all. We have business to do in this world yet ! The command to the Children of Israel is that they "Go Forward."

Now let us look at some of the promises to Jacob. In Gen. 28:13-15, we find the God of Abraham and of Isaac proclaiming Himself also the God of Jacob; there is the same promise of land: "To thee will I give it, and to thy seed." But, further, "Thou shalt spread abroad to the west, and to the east, and to the north, and to the south; and in thee and in thy seed shall all the families of the earth be blessed.'' (Combining once again the spiritual with the temporal). "And behold, I am with thee and will keep thee in all places whither thou goest, and will bring thee again into this land, for I will not leave thee, until I have done that which I have spoken to thee of.''

, These promises cannot be spiritualized away. The impression they made on Jacob himself is found in verse 20, 21: "If God will be with me, and will keep me in this way that I go, and will give me bread to eat, and raiment to put on, so that I come again to my father's house in peace; then shall the Lord be my God.''

The seed of Jacob was to spread to all points of the compass. Wandering Jews? No, but wandering Israelites for a long time. The "Blindness in part that is happened to Israel'' is greatly added to by the unwarranted confusion of the terms "Israelite'' and "Jew''; names which are never confounded in the Bible. None of the promises we have quoted so far were made to the Jews, though the Jews will have their proper part in them. Abraham was not a Jew, nor yet Isaac, nor Jacob, Joseph, Ephraim or Manasseh. Special promises were made to Judah, as we may see later, but it should always be borne in mind that only the House of Judah were Jews in a tribal sense; though portions of some of the other tribes, and the tribe of Levi, are believed to have thrown in their lot with Judah, and thus became Jews by religion. But our discussion deals mainly with the House of Israel, comprising the other ten tribes which never returned from the Assyrian captivity, and have been lost to human ken. This, the main branch of the children of Israel, known as the House of Israel, and spoken of in the Bible sometimes as "Israel,'' "Ephraim''. "Jacob'', "All Israel'', "The House of Joseph'', and "the Kingdom'', is never once referred to as "The Jews''; in fact, without a reference book at hand to consult, I believe I am right in saying that the House of Judah was never

called Jews until after the return to Jerusalem from the
Babylonian captivity; at which time of course the House
of Israel had disappeared into "the wilderness." Our
object is to advance proofs that the House of Israel is none
other than the Anglo-Saxon race of the British Empire,
and of the United States of America, for we by no means
ignore our blood relationship with the latter. Let us pass
on to the proofs.

Gen. 32: 28. "Thy name shall be called no more Jacob,
but Israel, for as a prince hast thou power with God and
with men, and hast prevailed." Israel, meaning a prince
or a ruler of God, was the fitting name chosen for the Head
of a great future power; not the Jews. They cannot be
held to have prevailed, nor to "have power"; and there is
no need for preachers to worry about finding explanations
as to why God's promises "to the Jews" could not be kept;
for the simple reason that these promises were not made to
the Jews. In passing, we should note that God's plan for
extending blessing to all nations of the earth, was not a
haphazard plan; it was to be placed in the hands of a people
of power, who were to push out to all points, north, south,
east and west. And all honor to the Church, all branches
of it, which conceived that the spreading of the gospel
was their special part of the plan. The Church has never
lagged far behind the flag; sometimes I am not sure that it
has not gone before !

Gen. 35: 11. "And God said unto him, I am God
Almighty; be fruitful and multiply; a nation and a company of nations shall be of thee, and kings shall come out
of thy loins." The forecast of a nation and a company
of nations is one of the strongest proofs of our identity.
It is plainly indicative of the British Empire, simply because
there exists no other power which fits the description of "a
nation and a company of nations." Canada, of course, has
her share in this.

CHAPTER IV

The passages of Scripture which we have been examining in these articles, and in which are foretold the blessings to be inherited by the Children of Israel, constitute a chain of evidence in support of the thesis that the Anglo-Saxons are none other than the long lost Ten Tribes of Israel.

The evidence is very strong, taken from either a positive or a negative viewpoint. On the positive side we find our proof in the fact that all the blessings and conditions foretold for the Children of Israel are now actually in possession of the British people, or are in a more or less advanced stage of fulfilment in and to the British, excepting only those promises which are specially the portion of Judah, or the Jews.

On the negative side the proof is equally strong, that no other race except the Anglo-Saxons are in possession of these blessings, or are at all likely to come into line for them. (For one must reflect that, before any other race could come into possession, the British Empire would have to be ousted from its position in the world, a thing impossible of accomplishment, desirable though it may seem to many of our contemporary renegades and malcontents, who are doomed to disappointment. The time set for ultimate fulfilment is too near at hand, and there is no other likely candidate in the field.) Supposing we had space to examine each of the nations of the earth, seeking by process of elimination to arrive at the people sought for, we would find at the end of our examination that there was left only the Anglo-Saxon race, for no other race fits into the picture, and since there must be such a people in existence, and our examination has left only the Anglo-Saxon race undiscarded, that race must necessarily be the race sought for. The principle of elimination so helpful in mathematical problems may be useful in this one. The reader might cast up in his mind a list of nations, and cancel off each nation to which all the descriptions do not apply, and note the result. (I am assuming that my good British reader is interested enough in his birthright to go to this trouble.)

So far we have seen that the nation foretold was to be the greatest, or "chief of the nations"; "a company of nations"; "possessing the gate of his enemy"; called in the name of Isaac; an evangelical nation, blessing the earth; and to be the possessor of the Scriptural "Land of Promise." Other conditions we shall notice later. Keep the elimination test in mind. **All these apply to the British, and they do not apply to any other people.**

In Genesis 48 we read the story of Jacob discharging his patriarchal task of passing on the birthright blessings to his rightful heirs. "And Jacob said unto Joseph, God Almighty appeared unto me at Luz in the land of Canaan and blessed me." It had happened long ago in his youth, but the secret had been his strength all his life long; and now that he was nearing death he must needs pass it on. And he made careful choice of his successors—"Now thy two sons, Ephraim and Manasseh are mine"—The others shall be thine, but these "are mine." There is no mistaking the significance of the choice; these were they who were to be prominent in subsequent history, and of these two, Ephraim was the chief. All the others were to be "called after the name of their brethren in their inheritance." Hence in later Scriptures we find the name of "Ephraim" used to designate not only the tribe of Ephraim, or Joseph, but the whole of the ten tribes of Israel, of which his was the leading or chief tribe. And so we read the quaint old story so faithfully recorded in a book which we call the

"Word of God," of an old man dying thousands of years ago and blessing his two grandsons, but why has it all been recorded and the account preserved throughout all the ages? Was it not because in that family death-bed scene was apportioned the destiny of the human race? Was it not Jacob's premonition of the mandate of Isaiah 54:2, 3. "Enlarge the place of thy tent, and let them stretch forth the curtains of thine habitations: spare not, lengthen thy cords, and strengthen thy stakes; for thou shalt break forth on the right hand and on the left; and thy seed shall inherit the Gentiles, and make the desolate cities to be inhabited"?

We see the choice of Ephraim before Manasseh when, by the deliberate crossing of his hands, Jacob placed his right hand on the head of Ephraim. Manasseh "also shall become a people, and he also shall be great; but truly his younger brother shall be greater than he, and his seed shall become a multitude of nations." The Anglo-Israelites of the United States are quite agreed that Ephraim represents the British, and Manasseh the American branch of the Anglo-Saxon race, but not all are ready to accept the allotment of relative greatness here assigned. The question "who should be greatest" still comes up between brothers, and we all have a weakness for that distinction, but the weight of evidence is preponderantly in favor of the British "company of nations," in possession of the "Land of Promise," etc. "Joseph is a fruitful bough, whose branches run over the wall." The birthright race is not contained within one set of boundaries; it is the race which has planted its flag all over the earth, and whose territory extends and is ever to expand "unto the utmost bound of the everlasting hills." (Read Genesis 49: 25, 26.) The only people to whom such language could apply are the British of Great and Greater Britain. It certainly would not apply to the United States of America, in their "splendid isolation." It is the British flag, and the British flag alone, which floats in every clime.

It is the British Empire alone which is ever extending to
the uttermost bounds of the earth. It occurs to the writer
that Jacob in his prophetic vision must have had a glimpse
of the great unknown world of the West; his words, "the
utmost bound," would refer to regions beyond the then
known world, far and away removed from the land of
Egypt in which he lay. The "everlasting hills" would include the Rockies of North America, in their majestic
grandeur and silent solitude, waiting for the time when
they were to be claimed as the heritage of the sons of
Joseph, whose branches were to run over the wall, to
"establish the earth," and to "inherit the desolate heritages," as the Anglo-Saxons, and they only, have done.
Judah is out of the question here. They (the Jews) have
not "established the earth," and their portion of the "land
of Promise" in Palestine is well defined, and not to be described as extending to the "utmost bound of the everlasting
hills." Thus are the Jews eliminated; but indeed all controversy on this point must stop at the Word of God, for
we read in I. Chron. 5 that "the birthright was Joseph's."
How could it then be Judah's? We must not look for fulfilment of these promises to the Jews.

Yet though Ephraim was set before Manasseh, they
were both set apart for special blessings, for "the birthright was given to the sons of Joseph." So both were
blessed—"And he blessed them that day, saying, In thee
shall Israel bless, saying, God make thee as Ephraim and as
Manasseh: and he set Ephraim before (not over) Manasseh."
Here we forge another link in the chain of evidence. The
Children of Israel were to be represented by two related
and independent people; the "great people" of Manasseh,
and the "greater than he" of Ephraim. Once again, the
Anglo-Saxon race, British and American, is the only race
fulfilling this condition. And Ephraim was set before
Manasseh. Nor is it unknown to history how the British

Ephraim has always gone before Manasseh in the matter of accepting the responsibilities imposed on the people who were to "establish the earth." The late war saw Ephraim again in the van; while Manasseh hung back for three years. We have seen British Ephraim driving the Turk from the Holy Land, and then accepting the mandate for its government. "Accepting the mandate" from the powers! That mandate which Britain inherited from the God of Abraham. That mandate which she had won by the prowess of her own troops. Accepting it from the powers. O modest Ephraim! Meanwhile Manasseh, in his wisdom, has refused the mandate for Armenia; Manasseh would fain hold himself aloof from the rest of the world, behind a screen known as the Monroe Doctrine—an altogether non-Israelitish conception. And so we must eliminate the United States Manasseh, **not from the relationship, but from the leadership.** That sort of leadership could never achieve the destiny appointed for Ephraim.

Here again we point to a most remarkable proof of our identity. See Isaiah 49:20—"The children which thou shalt have **after thou hast lost the other** shall say again in thine ears, The place is too strait for me; give place to me that I may dwell." The birthright sons of Joseph were to be a people who should lose one branch of their children. Even as Britain and the United States were separated. And the children to come after were again to say, the place is too strait for me, give place to me that I may dwell. (It will be noted that this passage is addressed to a Mother Country, in a superior position to the "child" which she was to lose; so is our position of leadership confirmed.) And it was even so that Great Britain, the "tight little island," "too strait" to contain its mighty race, was to become the Greater Britain of the British Empire.

Chatham, who felt so keenly the loss of the American Colonies, as we read in his dying speech—when he "rejoiced that he was still alive to lift up his voice against the dismemberment of this 'ancient and noble monarchy,' '' could he now get a view of the map of the world, blazed with the badge of the mighty Empire which has evolved, he might use the words of Isaiah 49:21: ''Who hath begotten me these, seeing I have lost my children, and am desolate.......... Behold, I was left alone: these, where had they been ?''

CHAPTER V.

In Genesis 49:1—Jacob, when he was dying, called his sons around him. "Gather yourselves together, that I may tell you that which shall befall you in the last days." What follows is Jacob's last will and testament. The dying patriarch was in full possession of his faculties, and the last words of this dying man are necessarily very important.

We have already considered some of the terms of Jacob's "will." Note especially, he was telling them what should befall them in the last days. Now, most theologians agree that the "last days," or the "latter days," as other scriptures have it, mean the Christian dispensation, that is the days of Anno Domini, since the birth of Christ and extending up to His second advent, yet in the future. Students of prophecy are also agreed that we are now very near the end of the "latter days," or, as one writer puts it, we are in the Saturday night of that period. Jacob's prophecy, then, would apply to the "last days" of the "latter days," or to the period of time through which we are now passing. Hence it follows that most of the prophecies have already been fulfilled. This is one of our strongest points. If not already fulfilled, they cannot be fulfilled at all ! That is to say, those prophecies which would necessarily occupy a long period of time, such as the gathering together of the scattered Israelites into a great nation, the House of Joseph; its subsequent re-division into the two independent nations representative of Ephraim and Manasseh; the still later "establishing of the earth." How ? By colonization and civilization surely, such as has taken place in the making of the British Empire; and, finally, the development of Ephraim into "a nation and company of nations," which, as we have seen, must be the British Empire, and which brings us up to the present time. All these were epochal developments, which could not be left until the "Saturday night" for fulfilment. We British-Israelites, are considered "fanciful," because we naturally conclude that these predictions, from the very nature of them, must have already been fulfilled, and we do not see where they have been fulfilled outside of the British Empire. Our opponents, and we have some amongst our own people, one of whom wrote a silly pamphlet called "British-Israel Foolishness," in which he showed that he was not even a Bible student; these are the "fanciful" ones on whom rests the onus of proof that the British Empire will have to be ousted within the next few years, and the whole process enacted all over again, including the formation of a nation and a company of nations; the expulsion of the British usurpers from the Holy Land, much to the disappointment of the Jews; the wiping out of the record of evangelization accomplished by the British and Foreign Bible Society; the re-arrangement of mankind under a new and better ideal. What ideal? Bolshevism? There is nothing else in sight. Is that better than British Imperialism? Well, it is the only alternative. Shall we re-unite under that? Now I submit that these are the people who are "seeing things."

What prophecies remain to be fulfilled, then, are those which can be fulfilled within a comparatively very short space of time. We may look for vivid and spectacular fulfilments now, because it is the "Saturday night," and they must take place before the Sunday morning of the Millennial period. We have already seen some of the spectacular events of the "last days." We saw how the British nation, with its "contemptible army" of imperishable fame, leaped,

all unprepared, into the breach for civilization We saw
how the sleeping giant shook himself, and, in the phrase of
Lloyd George, "struck mighty blows which sent autocrats
reeling from their thrones," when a non-military and industrial race took the field eight million strong; when all
the "company of nations" in the British Empire rallied to
the flag, and finally within four years defeated the machinery of the greatest military combine the world has ever
seen; a power whose business in all its branches, scientific
and industrial, was suborned to the ends and schemes of
militarism and conquest during forty years of studied preparation. We saw also the Americans finally throwing off
their cherished traditions of aloofness and joining hands
with their brethren. This last was not the least of the
phenomena, but it was only Manasseh unconsciously falling
into line with Ephraim; for blood will always tell. "They
are the ten thousands of Ephraim, and they are the thousands of Manasseh." It would never do for these to be
always separated. And they are to unite again, according
to the prophet Ezekiel, in a union not spasmodic but lasting.
This must be so unless a great many qualified students of
prophecy are mistaken. It will surely be one of the spectacular events of the "Saturday night." We may find
time to examine Ezekiel's prophecy in this connection later
on.

Again, let us notice that it is all about the "gathering
time" of which Jacob speaks in his last words. There is
nothing about the scattering time. And this is easily understood when we bear in mind that he is telling of what
is to befall them in the "last days," or towards the end of
the Christian era. Whereas the scattering time was to
take place long before Christ. It was about the year 975
before Christ that Israel was divided into two houses; the
House of Israel under King Jeroboam, and the House of
Judah, under Rehoboam. The House of Israel was taken

captive into Assyria about B.C. 721, and the House of Judah into Babylon in B.C. 606. The House of Israel never returned from the Assyrian captivity, but were subsequently scattered abroad, for they did not remain in Assyria. Later on we shall try to trace where they went, but for the present, we only note that it is the blessings, and the re-union in the latter days, of which Jacob prophesies in this prediction of the greatness which was to be the destiny of the sons of Joseph.

In this connection, let us examine the prophecy of Moses, also in his last words. He has a blessing for each of the twelve tribes. (Who says the ten tribes are lost and cast off forever?) Note the peculiarity of his prayer for Judah—"Hear Lord the voice of Judah, **and bring him unto his people.**" Bring him unto his people ? Now Judah was right there with his people at the time; so the prayer was a prophetic one in a vision extending to some time in the future when Judah should be separated from his people. But, bring **Judah** to his people ? Why not pray for the poor ten tribes, who were not only to be scattered but lost ? They were to lose sight of their identity; while the Jews, though scattered also, are always known; they have never been lost. Why pray specially for the Jews to be brought to their people ? Now that would be hard to understand did we not believe that Judah's people, his relatives, were to be a people of power, strongly established in the earth, able and willing to protect him, and under whose flag he would be free from the persecution he suffers, in Russia for instance, where he is not with his people. The Jews in the British Empire, and in the United States are free, and many of them prosperous. They have come to their people. They are not a nation, but citizens of many nations. With no country of their own, "their hands" were to be "sufficient for them"; and, incidentally, one notices that a Jew is generally able to make a living, when dwelling with his own people; you don't see many of them on the alms list; their hands are sufficient for them. They do not claim any country to be their national home, except the land of Palestine, which is yet, to them, a "Land of Promise." They cannot all go there, of course, but they will go there in a representative sense; and when they do, the striking fact must be noticed, they will be fulfilling the prophetic prayer of Moses, for the British flag flies over Jerusalem, and Judah must needs go "to his people." His people are the strong House of Joseph, with Ephraim the leader. The reader should look up Deut. 33, verses 13 to 17. This is Moses' blessing for Joseph, and it will be noted that it far surpasses anything foretold for the other tribes; yet all the ten tribes are included in this, for Ephraim, the leader, combines the whole House of Israel. "His glory is like the firstling of his bullock, and his horns are like the horns of unicorns: with them he shall push the people together to the ends of the earth: and they are the ten thousands of Ephraim, and they are the thousands of Manasseh." It will be some push, when Ephraim and Manasseh come to push together !

British-Israelites, who are keen students of heraldry, point out that the unicorn is incorporated in the royal arms of Britain. I wonder why ? Also the lion of the tribe of Judah ? But there is another point, and here I must refer to the text-book "British-Israel Truth," already quoted from. (In these articles, I have been using only the Bible as my text-book, telling the story as I have learned it, to fit the comprehension of ordinary work-a-day people, who don't know any more of the languages than I do.) I have quoted from the text-book the origin of the latter part of our race name, the word "Saxon." Now, as to the first part of it; I find the following: "**The Hebrew word 'Engl' or 'Angl'**................is used of speed and rapid movement: in the Bible phrases 'To skip like a calf,—

'Ephraim is a heifer that is taught'—and again, Ephraim is compared to a bullock unaccustomed to the yoke—in each case, for 'heifer,' 'calf,' or 'bullock,' the Hebrew word 'Angel' or 'Engl' is used. The root meaning is 'to speed swiftly'............ To be God's Messenger running swiftly to and fro bearing the Word of Life, was Israel's appointed work.'' Thus far the text-book. It is nice to know the languages ! Now we know about our own names, and they are all of Hebrew origin. ''Brit-ish'' —Covenant-People. ''Anglo-Saxons'' Messengers-Isaac's-Sons. All traced to the Hebrew. Interesting, isn't it ? Does anyone imagine it is all coincidence ?

CHAPTER VI.

In the song of Moses—Deut. 32:8-9—we read: "When the Most High divided to the nations their inheritance, when he separated the sons of Adam, he set the bounds of the people according to the number of the children of Israel. For the Lord's portion is his people; Jacob is the lot of his inheritance."

What mystery lies behind the phrase "separated the sons of Adam": who they were, or from whom they were separated, need not concern us in this examination. The thought which is uppermost is, that the Divinity, who is the Great Arbiter of human destiny, had a set plan of government for this world; and in the working out of His plan, by human agencies, He saw fit to appoint the Children of Israel to the premier position. It is not possible that the British race could have attained, in these latter days, to its pre-eminent place had they not been the people chosen by God to carry out His plan of government.

We make no pretence of having sounded the depths of the mystery of the Divine plans; but in studying this passage the thought is borne in upon us that when "the Most High set the bounds of the people according to the number of the children of Israel," He did so in exercise of His Divine prerogative, according to His own will, and for His own purpose; and since His declared will and purpose is that all nations might be blessed, then it follows that no nation or people in God's creation has a right to feel aggrieved that one race should be chosen as human agents to carry out His good will. It also follows that it would be poltroonery and ingratitude on the part of the

Children of Israel did they demur at their high calling. A vast burden of responsibility, it is true, is entailed on the British race by reason of their control of a world-wide empire; but are not the British peoples, nevertheless, in a far happier, more prosperous and enviable position than those of any other race ? A moment's reflection will furnish the answer to this question.

Yet, through ignorance no doubt, through indifference, through false humility, through failure to study God's Word as an up-to-date treatise on human affairs should be studied, we have our "Little Englanders," our hide-bound "Nationalists," our "conscientious objectors," and our rattle-headed Socialists, whose theory, forsooth ! is "Liberty, Equality, Fraternity," and whose practice is 'Bolshevism," and "The Reign of Terror." So arrogant in their wide narrowness, they would subjugate all mankind into acceptance of their conception of "good government"; and red death to those who oppose them. They would be the thinkers for all, and all should be forced to fall in with their thought-out plans. They would deny the right of the Most High to "set the bounds of the people." "The will of the people," they say, "is supreme"; and they, of course, are "the people." They would standardize the human race, destroying all individuality and trampling under foot all liberty. But, opposed to all this is the Word of God, calm and inscrutable, which states that He has set the bounds of the people according to a certain people chosen to carry out His will: and in compliance with the will of God only can have come into being this great Empire, whose sphere of influence is world-wide, and whose much-maligned imperialism is but the desire that oppressed and enslaved peoples should be granted protection, education, enlightenment, and stable government. This is the aim of British Imperialism. It is the prayer which breathes in the song of Empire, "God, who made thee mighty, make thee

mightier yet!'' The text we are considering, then, indicates
that God's plan of Government would place in the hands of
one race a wide-reaching dominance in the world's affairs.
This is the position held, and held only, by the British Empire; additional proof that Britain is''Israel''—God's Ruler.

In olden times there were those who cursed Jacob.
Did we require that for a sign ? Unfortunately, we have
it ! The British are the best-hated and most profusely
cursed race of people on earth. Anti-Britishers should
study the interesting lines of Numbers, Chap. 23 and 24.
They might there find light on the puzzle as to why such a
well-cursed people should apparently be in the enjoyment
of the blessings of a beneficent Providence. ''How shall
they curse whom God hath not cursed ? or defy, whom
God hath not defied ?'' Good Britishers should read these
chapters, too, and take courage. Balaam was hired to
curse, but he was forced to bear in mind the blessings
which God had poured out on Jacob, and he was compelled
to remind Jacob's enemy that ''God is not a man that he
should lie; neither the son of man, that he should repent;
hath he said, and shall he not do it ? or hath he spoken,
and shall he not make it good ? Behold, I have received
commandment to bless: and he hath blessed; and I cannot
reverse it.'' Here is plain warning to our enemies that
all their cursing is vain. ''Surely there is no enchantment
against Jacob, neither is there any divination against
Israel.'' Why ? Because ''The Lord his God is with him,
and the shout of a king is among them.''

And ''It shall be said of Jacob and of Israel, What
hath God wrought !'' Even as we, if we have any vision
at all, must reflect on the marvellous history of our dear
Motherland, and the phenomenon of the Empire race which
has its origin in the British Isles, a speck on the map, so
insignificant to look at, and so unassailable. When we
reflect on the vicissitudes of that history, the dangers

passed, the crises we have "blundered through," we can only say in amazement: What hath God wrought! And this very thing has been said by men who were qualified to speak as our nation's representatives; and by the men who were in the very best possible position to judge as to whether our deliverance from destruction was of God or of our own achievement. When I look up my English history for the story of the defeat of the Spanish Armada, I find extracts from Drake's despatch on the dispersion of the Spanish fleet "wonderful great and strong"—"Never anything pleased me better than seeing the enemy fly with a southerly wind to the north." Everybody knows the story of God's destruction of the Spanish Armada; but I wonder how many people connect that "What God wrought," which it was prophesied should be said of Jacob, with the inscription which was engraved on the medal struck in commemoration of Britain's deliverance from the then mighty Spain; the inscription read, "The Lord sent His wind and scattered them"—in short, "What hath God wrought!" Again, when the greatest military genius in history laid the whole of Europe at his feet, it was England alone which remained unconquered, and it was as a prisoner he "invaded" Britain. One most remarkable fulfilment of this prophecy occurred in 1914. It was at the time when the Germans, in the first flush of their might, were advancing on Paris, and they swerved aside for some reason that has never been explained by anyone but Lord Roberts. And Lord Roberts, it will be admitted, was a strategist qualified to judge what our chances were, had the German advance continued at that time. It was reported in the Daily Chronicle that Lord Roberts was sitting with Kitchener when the telegram announcing the sudden retreat of the Germans was handed in; and Lord Roberts' exclamation was, "**Only God Almighty could have done this.**" What hath God wrought!

Meanwhile, the cursing goes on apace; and the British Lion once again is couchant; the world's greatest example of national patience. But not for always, it seems, if this prophecy is to be fulfilled, and who can doubt it? For "His seed shall be in many waters"—"He hath, as it were, the strength of an unicorn: he shall eat up the nations his enemies, and shall break their bones, and pierce them through with his arrows. He couched, he lay down as a lion, and as a great lion: who shall stir him up? Blessed is he that blesseth thee, and cursed is he that curseth thee." These are re-assuring chapters for Britishers to read at such times as they feel weary of the nightmare of slander and cursings to which our race is being subjected. The whole of the chapters are prophetic of the latter days, that is, of our days. See Chap. 24: 14. "Come, therefore, and I will advertise thee what this people shall do to thy people **in the latter days."** Sons of Balak take heed.

The British are the only people whose seed are in many waters, and the possessors of "the ships that shall come from the coast of Chittim." Once again, the Jews, who are the recognized seed of Jacob, cannot be indicated here, because they are in no position to mete out destruction to their enemies. The seed of Jacob, of whom this is foretold, must, therefore, be the lost tribes. All the prophecies point in our direction.

CHAPTER VII.

Perhaps the reason why people do not study Old Testament Scripture more is their failure to realize what a wonderfully up-to-date book the Old Testament is. The symmetry of Holy Writ is lost on those who confine their reading to the New Testament; I hardly think the great truths of the New Testament can be fully grasped without a good practical knowledge of the writings of the inspired prophets which it confirms. The Bible is an inexhaustible mine; the deeper you dig, the better you are rewarded. But again, there is a vast deal of truth that you do not have to dig very deep for—it stares you in the face. People do not see it because they are imbued with an idea that they must look only for spiritual meanings in everything, while they overlook the fact that the spiritual and literal meanings of all prophecies are correlative; as also are both books of the Bible. What spiritual value can any prophecy have, if the prophecy itself be not destined to fulfilment? What spiritual value, for instance, would prophecies about the birth and atoning death of Christ, our Redeemer, have, if these stupendous events were not to take place? If you do not believe in the literal birth, death and resurrection of our Lord, it is very evident that you cannot get any spiritual benefit therefrom. Here nobody denies that the spiritual and the literal are inter-dependent. But this applies to all inspired prophecy. Yet to most people the greater part of the Bible doesn't really mean what it says; it means something else; and preachers, yes, most of them, good Christians as they are, handle Old Testament records as if they were interesting curios of a by-gone time, from the contemplation of which, by some stretch of the imagination, we might draw useful lessons for everyday life.

To give, as an illustration, just one instance that I have fresh in mind—I went to hear an eloquent preacher; and when he announced his text—about the building of Jerusalem on its own heap—I was on the "qui-vive" for new views. But he closed his Bible and preached a sermon all about building up character from the ruins of morals; very well in its way, but it had nothing, except by stretch of imagination, to do with the subject of the text. This, however, is quite the usual way in which these prophetic passages of Scripture are treated; and how Christians can take the pronouncements of the Bible appertaining to the restoration of "The Kingdom," to God's dealings with His ancient people, "The lot of His inheritance," to His designs for the world's destiny, and whittle them down to merely another way of saying that young men and young women of our day should give up the tobacco habit and the powder puff, passes comprehension. It is more than pitiable. Bible prophecies are nothing less than histories of future events. This can be realized only when we realize that they are the enunciations of the great I Am. We are surely attaching an overweening importance to ourselves, and our own generation, do we imagine that these eternal verities are to be adjusted to our modern thought, or that they are mere rules and examples laid down especially with a view to our edification, to be modified and toned down, should we fail to find time, or lack inclination to devote a due amount of our thought to them. The tide of God's decrees will carry us on in any case. Now, in my opinion, the brand of "spiritual" meaning that is usually drawn from Old Testament prophecies has not one thousandth part of the spiritual uplift that would result from an expounding of the literal meanings; so that young scions of our ancient race might know who they are, where they are in the eternal scheme of things, and what part they are expected to play in reference to what is happening all around them in these "latter days"; that they might shape their lives and characters according to the correctness of their information, and the fulness of their knowledge of the unsearchable riches of the Word of God. "Noblesse Oblige" does not spell eternal salvation, but it certainly should lend force to the platitudes of moral philosophy. It should not be ignored by those whose special office it is to point high standards of character and ideal. If the Word of God be all true, then we need it all; for, after all, it is the Truth which shall make us free. I have said this is my opinion; but it is the opinion of every British-Israelite; for our pride is that we stand for the vindication of the whole Word of God, Old Testament and New.

And what shall the Truth set us free from? Well, from ignorance, for one thing; and from the danger of being confused and carried away by crude doctrines, or being caught in the vortex of the ominous movements that are rife in the world in these our times.

Amongst the sinister movements of these "latter days", we must reckon with Bolshevism, now definitely aligned with the enemies of our Empire. In our last article, which took in consideration of the trade-marks of the enemies of Jacob, I drew a pen picture of Bolshevism; and a few days later it was confirmed word for word by Lenine, the Russian high priest of the conspiracy; that uncouth being who has stalked on to the world's stage—quite possibly that the Scripture might be fulfilled.

Lenine (according to the Montreal Gazette cable, Sept. 11, 1920) has written a letter to the French Socialist newspaper, "Humanite," laying down conditions under which Socialists are to be admitted to the "Third Communist Internationale of Moscow." He rather upbraids the Socialists for lack of co-operation; and then he tells just what Bol-

shevism means. He says: "You talk and talk about joining
the Third Internationale. Do you know what that means ?
It means Red Revolution with Blood and Fire" (Red death,
I called it, but this is near enough.) "It means martyrdom
and persecution" (Outlaws are very prone to pose as martyrs). "It means the formation by you of a Communist party
on Russian lines, which shall own full allegiance to Moscow,
and accept my decrees as infallible" (He has done all the
thinking). "It means, the day of half measures is past,
and the waverers must be expelled. Thus, and thus alone,
can our goal of world revolution be achieved."

This is Lenine's own definition of his aims. His goal
is "World Revolution." But athwart the schemes of
Bolshevism lies the British Empire, established by the
Covenant of the Almighty. Those who are not with Lenine,
he says, are against him. Well, British-Israelites are against
him and his "International" first, last and always ! Those
who deprecate British Imperialism should consider well the
situation. The antithesis of British Imperialism is separate
Nationalism. How is Nationalism equipped to oppose the
"Internationalism" of Lenine and his socialist coterie ?
How long would Nationalism survive if betrayed by traitors
from within, who would lay their respective nations at the
feet of Lenine, the would-be international world-ruler ?
These are questions for those, so independent people, whose
sentiments are opposed to the instincts of union for mutual
help, which is the basic idea of British Imperialism. Granted that those to whom this appeal is made would not will-
ingly surrender their respective national entities to the
Bolshevist autocrat of democracy in Moscow, how are they
prepared to defend themselves against traitors from within,
whose low-born views take no cognizance of anything beyond materialism, and the aggrandizement of their own
class and generation ? One often hears vague reference
to "the dangers of Imperialism"; but there is danger every-

where. **Argumentum ad hominem !** We are only safe, we are only free, within our own Empire, and under our own flag.

This may all seem like digression, but not so; our subject, this part of it, is consideration of what is to befall us in the "latter days," and I would emphasize that, although, as the lady put it, we may spend a little extra time with Moses in the bulrushes, it is an up-to-date study which gives a true perspective of the dangers foretold as besetting our Empire in the "latter days." Nor is it drawing a long bow, to assert that Bolshevism is one of these dangers. We have just seen how an English socialist newspaper was supplied with $350,000 of Bolshevist money for propaganda purposes in England. It was also announced some time ago that a large sum of this unclean money was diverted to aid Sinn Fein in Ireland; $500,000, I think, was the figure named. So that loud-mouthed and lofty-phrasing set of hypocrites and murderers, self-styled "martyrs and patriots," would lay their country at the feet of Lenine, in their blind and inveterate hatred of Britain (The Covenant-Land), at whose hand they have received every benefit that good government could devise; in which government they are privileged to participate, and under which they enjoy an extent of liberty unknown in any other land or under any other government in this world. Britain received a mandate to rule in righteousness, and in no other country within the Empire is that mandate more faithfully and generously discharged than it is in Ireland. Sinn Fein, in the monstrosity of its moral obliquity, the world's greatest example of public mendacity, may well line itself up with the Russian Bolsheviki. Are they not the spiritual descendants of Balak, who hired Balaam to curse Israel ? Quite possibly they are his literal descendants. We know they are of Eastern, Phoenician stock; I doubt if they are true Celts. And when Balaam, "The man whose eyes were

open," and who "knew the knowledge of the Most High,"
"advertised" Balak of the things which "this people shall
do to **thy people** in the latter days," we may justly draw
two conclusions: First, that the people, or descendants of
Balak, are to be found amongst our enemies; and, second,
that there is retribution in store for them.

The Prophet Daniel tells of the King of the North,
and Ezekiel of Gog, as coming up against Israel in the last
days. Now Gog is believed to be Russia. I would not
pose as an alarmist, but it may be that the rising tide of
Bolshevism portends the gathering of the forces which are
to dispute the rulership of the world with Israel on the
battlefield of Armageddon. The powers opposed to us, according to Britsh-Israel authorites, will probably include
the hordes of the old Assyrian, Babylonian. Persian, Grec-
ian, Roman, and Ottoman Empires. There is no manner
of doubt but that an attempt will be made to overthrow
the British Empire, and the time cannot be very far distant.
It will be a time of stress and trial; but those who are
cognizant of British-Israel truth are full of thankful confidence; for we believe that God means exactly what He
says: "Alas ! for that day is great, so that none is like it;
it is even the time of Jacob's trouble; but he shall be saved
out of it, and they will serve the Lord their God and David
their King, whom I will raise up unto them." (Jer. 30:7,
and Ezekiel 37:24).

In this chapter we have gone ahead considerably in
order to demonstrate that the prophetic books of the Bible
are an up-to-date study, and not to be taken as mere alle-
gories. In our next we shall return to further consideration of our identification marks.

CHAPTER VIII.

From very early in the history of God's ancient people, the Twelve Tribes of Israel, we find they were regarded by Him as made up of two nationalities. See, for instance, Psalm 114:1, 2. "When Israel went out of Egypt . . . . Judah was his sanctuary, and Israel his dominion." Yet, by a strange lack of perception, most people read such passages as this without noticing the division of the chosen people into two parts, two houses, two nationalities; which, though closely related in blood, and identical in history up to a certain period, were, in pursuance of God's will, and for the consummation of His purpose, to be rent apart, sundered and separated, both in location and in history. The one part, the House of Joseph, or "Israel," to be divorced from the conditional Mosaic covenant, and to be Gentilized, scattered abroad; to become "Lo-ammi"—not God's people—during many centuries, but through the Love and Faithfulness of God, to become Christianized and redeemed, brought back to their relationship with God by the merits of their Redeemer, into their ancient heritage under the everlasting Abrahamic covenant of grace and to enjoyment of the temporal blessings promised to their forefathers; which promises, vouched by the oath of Jehovah, cannot be broken, and are no less sure of fulfilment than are the spiritual blessings inherited by those who become joint heirs with Christ by virtue of their faith in His atonement.

The other part, the House of Judah, were to remain faithful in their endeavour, however vain, to keep, in the letter if not in the spirit, the Mosaic law; only to become a living national example of the utter futility of mankind

to hope to measure up to the standard of righteousness
which man would have to attain in order, by his own efforts,
to meet the requirements of the Most Holy One of Israel.
And by their continued rejection of God's substitute, by
their crucifixion of His Christ, whose blood they invoked
as a curse on their own heads and on their children, to
remain under the curse of the broken law; scattered, despised among the nations, in non-enjoyment of any of the
temporal blessings of the Abrahamic covenant; and so to
remain until the time happily prophesied for them also,
when they shall look upon Him whom they have pierced,
and accepting Him, the one great Mediator between an
outraged God and His creatures, shall bow the knee and
the heart to Him, and fully partake of the long-deferred
blessings promised to their nation under the unaltered
Abrahamic covenant of grace.   The redemption of the
House of Judah will not be until then; and that time will
be the millennium.

The essential difference between the Mosaic and the
Abrahamic covenants should always be borne in mind.
They are utterly distinct. The Mosaic covenant was the
law given by Moses, one must conclude, to fasten on man
the conviction of his guilt, and his utter inability to save
himself. Doubtless, if man could keep the law, he would
be saved by the law; but it was impossible for fallen man
to keep a law which could be broken even by a wrong
thought. We read "The thought of foolishness is sin."
That was enough to convict Saint Paul of his guilt, for
even he could not keep the rigor of that law; "When the
commandment came, sin revived, and I died." But Christ
is Himself the fulfilment of the law to all such as believe.
That the Abrahamic covenant of grace, and the Mosaic
covenant or law, are entirely different is plainly stated in
Deut. 5: 2. "The Lord made a covenant with us in Horeb.
The Lord made not this covenant with our fathers, but

with us, even with us." That covenant was conditional on
our obedience; and we have broken it. But, thanks to
a faithful God, the anterior covenant of grace remains,
ratified by the New Covenant. And Christ—let me repeat
it for the benefit of those who fear that any thought directed to the temporal blessings would detract from allegiance
to Him—Christ is the personification of the New Covenant;
and all true British-Israelites, who have at all grasped the
fulness of the great revelation of their identity, know that
it is by His merits alone we can have come into the enjoyment, as a race, of those promises of our fathers' God, for
the integrity and faithful fulfilment of which we are so
insistent and so jealous. If King Solomon could say of the
Lord of "His people Israel" (I. Kings 8:56): "There hath
not failed one word of all His good promise," surely we are
justified in attesting the same truth. Certainly we have
no right and no cause to say anything else. The God of
Israel is the same yesterday, to-day, and forever. Christ
says: "I and My Father are One"; then surely the coming
of Christ, and His work of redemption, did not herald a
change of plan on the part of Him in whom there is no
variableness, neither shadow of turning. The original
promises remain, some fulfilled, some yet to be fulfilled.
This, then, is our faith in Christ and in God.

These thoughts lead up to realization of the fundamental fact that the early division of God's people into two
nations was an essential part of the profound plan of the
Almighty to accomplish the salvation of mankind. To put
it shortly, one branch of the children of Israel was to furnish the Saviour, and the other branch was to spread the
tidings. (Which we have been fully equipped and placed
in position to do.) It should be a fascinating study to try
and trace the wonderful workings of this plan, more especially now that we have indisputable proof that our own
race are, and have been, the chief actors in the great drama,

or rather the chief instruments in the hands of the Author of all.

Passing on from the patriarchal times to the kings, and from the prophetic to the historical passages (for in our running commentary we are forced to skip many interesting stopping places) we find that after the death of Saul, about the year B.C. 1050, David was anointed king over the House of Judah only: "The men of Judah came, and there they anointed David King over the House of Judah." . . . "The House of Judah have anointed me king over them" (2 Sam. 2:4, 7). And Saul's son, Ish-bosheth, was made king over "all Israel": "He began to reign over 'ISRAEL'. . . . But the HOUSE OF JUDAH followed David." Then, through successful intrigue, the two houses were brought under David's rule. But, though the kingship was temporarily fused, not so the people, for we read that "In Hebron he reigned over Judah seven years and six months; and in Jerusalem he reigned thirty and three years over ALL ISRAEL AND JUDAH."

Now we pass on to Solomon's reign, and, in I. Kings 11:9, 11-13, we read "The Lord was angry with Solomon," and said, "I will surely rend the KINGDOM from thee, and will give it to thy servant. Notwithstanding, in thy days I will not do it, for David thy father's sake; but I will rend it out of the hand of thy son. Howbeit, I will not rend away all the kingdom; but I will give one tribe to thy son for David, My servant's sake, and for Jerusalem's sake, which I have chosen." Observe here, it was the KINGDOM that was to be taken from Solomon's son. This is an interesting point. We find the House of Israel spoken of as "The Kingdom"; this same house referred to in Psalm 114 as the "Dominion," in distinction from Judah, the "Sanctuary." Later on, we see how the prophet Ahijah illustrated the matter to Jeroboam. "He laid hold of the new garment which was upon him and rent it in twelve pieces. And he said to Jeroboam: Take thee **ten pieces,** for thus saith the Lord, the God of Israel, behold, I will rend the KINGDOM out of the hand of Solomon, and will give ten tribes to thee; but he shall have one tribe for my servant David's sake, and for Jerusalem's sake. . . . Howbeit, I will not take the whole kingdom out of his hand, but I will take the kingdom out of his son's hand, and will give it unto thee, EVEN TEN TRIBES. And unto his son I will give one tribe, that David, My servant, may have A LAMP alway before me in Jerusalem." Here we see that God was not to take ten tribes out of Rehoboam's kingdom, but He was to take the kingdom from Rehoboam; and the kingdom was ten tribes. Also observe that, as ten and one make eleven only, we must conclude that the one tribe given to Rehoboam "as a lamp in Jerusalem," was to be in addition to the tribe over which David ruled originally, that is the tribe or house of Judah. Most writers also seem to agree that part of the tribe of Levi, the priestly tribe, went with Judah, and part remained with Israel. Whether very many of the tribe of Levi are now with Judah, and known as Jews, is a point on which the writer has seen no definite information. The point which is quite authentic, however, is that it was the tribe of Benjamin, Joseph's brother, which was given as "a lamp" or light-bearing tribe to Judah. And Benjamin's was a wonderful mission; for, as it turned out, this tribe was only loaned to Judah for a purpose; and, having accomplished this purpose of light-bearing to Judah, they were to continue and extend their mission as light-bearers to "the lost sheep of the House of Israel." It is believed that all the Apostles, with the exception of Judas Iscariot, were men of Galilee, of the tribe of Benjamin. Saint Paul also states that he was a Benjamite; thus did they fulfill their office as light-bearers. This does not, of course, mean that all Benjamin were converted to Christianity in Christ's time, though it is evident that most of His converts were of that tribe; while the Jews, "His own," for Christ was of the tribe of Judah, "received Him not." Benjamin, in fact, as a tribe, subsequently left Judah, and wandered after the other nine, or nine and a half, or ten tribes, whichever the correct count may be, and eventually reached HOME (their new home), leaving only Judah, and possibly some of Levi, to be now known to the world as "Jews." In our next chapter, we shall take up the story of the revolt, and subsequent scattering of the tribes.

CHAPTER IX.

After the death of Solomon, his son Rehoboam reigned over the houses of Judah and Israel; and Jeroboam, who had fled into Egypt to escape the jealousy of King Solomon, was now called upon by "the congregation of Israel" to head a deputation to the King with an appeal for leniency in taxation. "Thy father made our yoke grievous: now therefore make thou the grievous service of thy father, and his heavy yoke which he put upon us, lighter, and we will serve thee." That was the reasonable petition; and it would be hard to imagine a more unstatesmanlike answer than that given by the King, acting on the advice of his junker counsellors. "My father made your yoke heavy, and I will add to your yoke: my father also chastised you with whips, but I will chastise you with scorpions."

But a people like the Israelites, with the elements of greatness in their blood, could not brook such an insulting rebuff. Deep-grounded in the heart of the Israelite nation was the instinct of loyalty to the throne which can be seen in the terms of their petition: "We will serve thee." This is a trait also of the British character, which has been commented on at various times by many writers. The British have been loyal to all kinds of sovereigns, good, bad, and indifferent; impelled by a strain of psychology which runs in the blood, and dates from very ancient times. Everyone familiar with English history is aware of the struggles by which, from pre-Magna Charta days down to within comparatively recent years, the constitutional British Monarchy came to its birth. How tenaciously the British people have stuck to the plan of government by monarchy, and have refused the idea of republicanism ! There is a reason for this, and we shall see later that inborn loyalty to the crown was necessary that the scriptural promises might be fulfilled.   But this contemptuous insult was not to be borne by the Israelites; indeed it was expressly designed by God in order to bring about the revolt.   The bitterness of disappointment is noticeable in their rejoinder: "What portion have we in David? neither have we inheritance in the son of Jesse."   And their independent spirit is seen in the sharp decision: "To your tents O Israel: now see to thine own house, David."   So "Israel" departed to their tents; and from that day to this the houses of Israel and Judah have never been re-united.

That is the short story of the revolt.   Its nominal cause was an ordinary commonplace matter of domestic taxation, but it was the result of no chance of circumstance: behind it all was the hand of God, for, it is expressly stated, "It was a thing brought about of the Lord."   In any intelligent study of God's dealings with His chosen people it is necessary to grip the fact that He was shaping their course in accordance with His own fore-ordained plan; each episode must be considered in its relation to the course of destiny foretold for Israel. and if we interpret any of the Scriptural accounts relating to specific events, in a way contradictory to the prophetic passages governing the destiny of the people, we may rest assured that our interpretation is wrong. It is absolutely necessary to realize that there were no deviations from the plan, and no spasmodic changes en route.   Failure to bear this in mind has been more fruitful of misunderstanding of Scripture, than, perhaps, all other causes put together.   We have no ground whatever for assuming that God's plan has ever changed, or that it is not in operation now.   So accustomed have we become to thinking of God as the Deity of the spiritual world; to be worshipped in churches, in a spirit of mind duly divorced from mundane affairs. that we fail to realize as we ought, the fact that His hand still over-rules the destiny of our people, and things are still "brought about of the Lord." Yet it must be so; for surely God has made no miscalculations which would necessitate any alteration of His plan according as time developed and showed Him His mistakes. This must dispose of all the arguments of those whose line of theology, through devious roundabout ways, arrives at the uninspiring conclusion that, owing to Israel's sins God had to change His plan, and alter His original intention in regard to them. It was no part of God's plan for Israel that they should settle down in ease to enjoy good times. He had a purpose for them far other, and far elsewhere. This people were destined to be scattered far and wide, and to be re-gathered in another land which God had set apart for them, from which they were to be moved or driven out no more. (2 Sam. 7:10) "Moreover I will appoint a place for my people Israel, and will plant them, that they may dwell in a place of their own, and move no more; neither shall the children of wickedness afflict them any more, as beforetime."

But He who had brought His people out of bondage in Egypt by miracles displaying His omnipotence; who had led them forty years through the wilderness by a pillar of fire and a cloud; had thrown down the walls of Jericho before them at the blast of a trumpet; surely He might have used thunder and lightning to rend the kingdom out of the hand of Rehoboam. But, no, it all happens naturally, a mere question of political economy. Does it not seem as if He had another of His attributes which He wished to impress upon His people to all generations, i.e., His omnipresence? We may be sure of it; things are "brought about of the Lord" just in that way in our own times. Can we reflect on the chaotic state of human affairs at the present time without realizing that it may be, no, that it must be "of the Lord" that half the world seems to have

gone crazy? Times are surely ripening for a great fundamental change. We see, day by day, the best and cleverest
minds strained to their utmost to devise schemes to stabi-
lize human affairs and restore the sanity of order; but
plan after plan fails to have its logical effect. "There's
a Divinity that shapes our ends, rough-hew them how we
will." We recently witnessed the spectacle of a great
nation of more than a hundred million people hanging on
the words of one man. who seemed to have conceived the
idea that the warring nations of Europe would pause to
listen to and weigh his logic; the faulty logic of President
Wilson, which took absolutely no account of the human
element. There was something wrong with the logic of
a man who, shut up in his private study, imagined that the
words, mere words, which he arranged in sets of "stately
phrases," would have such an effect on the "Imperial German Government" to which they were so decorously addressed, as to make them halt in their mid-career, relinquish their
cherished ambitions, and go back home to live in peace.
There was something wrong with the logic of the phrase-
making President who racked his brain to choose
certain words calculated to "make the world safe for
democracy," and usher in a period of universal peace. It
was the error of a mind suffering from the inexperience of
isolation. There was something wrong with the great people who looked to him as an oracle. It is not in the
prophecies that universal peace shall come about in that
way, by easy transition. There is another consideration;
there is a demonstration to be made. Before the warring
nations have come to the bitter end of their resources, there
is One who shall be recognized. "The nations shall know
that I am the Lord." They shall know it and admit it,
when it is forced on their understanding. That is a part
of the plan. It is in the prophecy. It has never been
changed. **It must be fulfilled.**

I was going to mention it somewhere in these studies, and may as well now. I wonder if God has anything to do with the League of Nations ? It doesn't seem to be a success so far, and there is nothing foretold about it in the Bible. If the affairs of the world were to be settled in that way in the "latter days" surely there would be a forecast of it somewhere in the Scriptures. Some years ago, before I had thought anything about our identity with the Ten Tribes of Israel, I remarked in writing to the press, that the British Empire itself comprised the only practical "League of Nations." I thought so then, and I am sure of it now. I believe the "company of nations" known as the British Empire, is "a thing brought about of the Lord," because it is plainly stated in the Bible that such a "company of nations" composed of one race of people should come into being in the latter days. But I have not seen anything about the child of President Wilson's brain—a League of Nations, comprising all the different races of the earth who cared to join it. Perhaps it is not "of the Lord"; it doesn't seem to fit in anywhere in the prophecies, which it surely should if it were destined to materialize. Nor does it harmonize with God's declaration of His choice of one people to carry out His will. It is of Israel we read in Jeremiah 51:20, "Thou art my battle axe and weapons of war: for with thee will I break in pieces the nations, and with thee will I destroy kingdoms." And then, in happier times, when the demonstration shall have been completed (We must not lose sight of any of the details of the plan) then, "Many nations shall come, and say, Come and let us go up to the mountain of the Lord, and to the house of the God of Jacob. Micah 4: 1, 4.

CHAPTER X.

After the revolt of the House of Israel, we read, in 1 Kings 12: 21, that Rehoboam "assembled all the House of Judah with the tribe of Benjamin . . . . to fight against the House of Israel, to bring back the kingdom again to Rehoboam the son of Solomon." But "Thus saith the Lord, ye shall not go up nor fight against your brethren the children of Israel: return every man to his house; for this thing is from me." I am trying to emphasize the truth, that the revolution was engineered by God, in ac-cordance with His over-ruling plan. This is the thread which appeals to me as running through the whole story.

Now when Jeroboam was made King over the House of Israel, he conceived a plan of his own to secure himself in his throne. His apprehensions laid hold of him; but he did not resort to prayer about it, and dedicate his king-ship to God, as every honest man placed in a great position of public trust ought to do. No, he communed in his heart —See 1 Kings, 12: 26-28, for what Rehoboam found it in his heart to do—"Whereupon the King took counsel, and made two calves of gold, and said unto them: "It is too much for you to go up to Jerusalem, behold thy gods, O Israel, which brought thee up out of the land of Egypt." So the children of Israel turned to idolatry. This was the sin which brought the anger of God down upon the House of Israel· It would appear from the verdict of scripture that the sin of idolatry is the most heinous crime that man is capable of committing; a direct insult to God, it is without excuse. Man by his fall became a prey to many evil passions and vices, which become a part of his depraved nature; but even in his fallen state man was expected to place his hope in God: the sin of idolatry, or dethroning

God, is unnatural even to fallen nature. We should give it a very wide berth.

God's judgment against Jeroboam and, sequentially, against the House of Israel, is pronounced in 1 Kings 14: "Thou hast gone and made thee other gods and molten images to provoke me to anger, and hast cast me behind thy back: Therefore, behold, I will bring evil upon the house of Jeroboam—For the Lord shall smite Israel as a reed is shaken in the water, and he shall root up Israel out of this good land which he gave to their fathers; and shall scatter them beyond the river." This prophecy of judgment against Israel was made about the year B.C. 956; and it was fulfilled in part between the years B. C. 741 and 676, during which period the people of the Northern Kingdom were taken captive in different relays into Assyria; and the fulfilment was completed when they subsequently left the land of their captivity, and wandered of their own accord "beyond the river" Euphrates, and scattered in various directions, as it was decreed and foretold that they should do.

By his wanton treachery Jeroboam earned for himself the title of "the man who made Israel to sin." In the short recital of the reigns of the succeeding eighteen kings of Israel, almost without exception, we find that "they did evil in the sight of the Lord," and it is monotonously chronicled that they "departed not from the sins of Jeroboam, the son of Nebat, who made Israel to sin." Their continuance in idolatry resulted in the piling up of the wrath of God against them: this took ominous shape in the reign of King Jehu, in whose days we read "the Lord began to cut Israel short." It was the beginning of the end. Now the enemies of Israel became, pro tem., the servants of God. "And God stirred up the spirit of Pul, King of Assyria, and the spirit of Tiglath-pileser, king of Assyria, and he carried them away, even the Reubenites

and the Gadites, and the half tribe of Manasseh, and
brought them into Halah, and Habor, and Hara, and to the
river Gozan, unto this day.'' (They never returned.)
This transportation was done piecemeal; it will not be
necessary to cite the long list of captives, but among less
familiar names, we find Gilead, and Galilee, and all the land
of Naphtali, carried captive to Assyria. The nineteenth
and last King of Israel was Hoshea: and "Against him
came up Shalmaneser, king of Assyria." . . . . "And the
Lord rejected all the seed of Israel, and afflicted them, and
delivered them into the hands of the spoilers, until he had
cast them out of his sight—Until the Lord removed Israel
out of his sight, as he had said by all his servants the
prophets. So was Israel carried away out of their own
land to Assyria unto this day. And the king of Assyria
brought men from Babylon, and from Cuthah . . . . and
placed them in the cities of Samaria instead of the children
of Israel: and they possessed Samaria, and dwelt in the
cities thereof." (The reader should note that Samaria,
the Northern province, was the province of Israel; while
Judea, the land of Judah, was the Southern province)·
From this account, in 2 Kings, 17, it is plain that the banishment was complete; not only were the Israelites dis-
possessed, but strangers were put in possession. Clearly
they were not intended to return. Now the Books of
Chronicles were written after the end of the Babylonian
captivity, when the Jews had returned to Judea; and in
1 Chronicles 5:26, we find the statement that those of the
Assyrian captivity were in exile "unto this day." Note
this fact carefully; it is forgotten sometimes, as we shall
see later on.

In 2 Kings, 18, we are informed just why the Israelites
were thus punished—"Because they obeyed not the voice
of the Lord their God, but transgressed His covenant, **and
all that Moses the servant of the Lord commanded.**" This is

a definite statement of the case against them. They were carried away captive because they transgressed the covenant made with Moses; in other words, the Law of Moses. The Abrahamic Covenant, based on the Oath of the covenant-keeping God, of course remains, unsullied and magnificent, as sure of fulfilment as it was on the day it was enacted. These Israelites could not break that Covenant; they were no party to it; they simply inherited its benefits as the seed of Abraham. Nevertheless, the Law of Moses was broken, by idolatry. This sin is compared in many scriptures with the sin of adultery; when they cast God behind them "My covenant they brake, although I was an husband unto them saith the Lord." By this simile we get a glimpse of what manner of love God has for His chosen people! But now they were uncovenanted, they divorced themselves; 'they became Lo-ammi, not God's people, until their redemption by Christ, through whom they were re-covenanted. At the period under discussion, however, they were uncovenanted, and "not God's people," and their condition as such has a direct bearing on some of the wrong theories held by people who have not, as I take it, made as profound a study of the scriptures as they imagine they have. It is an immense mistake when people approach this great study with a preconceived theory of their own, and try to explain away, or ignore altogether as "difficult passages," those parts of God's Word which will not fit in with their theory. The better way is to reject theories that call for a readjustment of the Word of God. We may not be able to comprehend all of His plan, but we ought to know that it is not to be adjusted to suit our capacity, or to bring it in line with our ideas of things as they ought to be.

One of these theories, very commonly accepted, involves as its sequence that all the wonderful promises of the greatness of the House of Joseph, the birthright tribe, came to a miserable end, and failed entirely of accomplishment. Of course that sequence is not emphasized by the theorists, but that is exactly what it amounts to. The theory is that the Ten Tribes returned to Jerusalem with the House of Judah, when part of the latter returned from Babylonian captivity, and that they became absorbed with Judah, and are now known as Jews. This theory, involving as it does the corollary of a denial of all prophecies, is very widely accepted. Why ? I don't know. Possibly most people don't bother to read the prophecies, and many who do, take them with a pinch of salt. Under this theory, there is no "chief of the nations," no "company of nations," nothing of anything that we do not see possessed by the Jews ; and the Jews, as a people, are in possession of nothing. Is that a fulfilment of the covenant promises, and the covenant oath ? It is not. And it is a direct contradiction of 1 Chron. 5 : 26, which I have called attention to. I have just been reading a critical review of a book, written by an English clergyman, in which this theory is propounded. The reviewer is one of the able editors of "The Banner of Israel." He dwells considerably on what the author evidently regarded as his strongest point; but it would hardly take such a thorough Bible student as Mr. Taylor to dispose of it. The piece-de-resistance of the book is the passage in Ezra 1:5: "Then rose up the chief of the fathers of Judah and Benjamin, and the priests, and the Levites, with all them whose spirit God had raised, to go up to build the house of the Lord which is in Jerusalem." The grand contention being that the phrase "All them whose spirit God had raised" must necessarily include the Ten Tribes! Of course it was easy to dispose of this theory, in view of the fact (1) That the Ten Tribes had been divorced from the temple worship, and the Mosaic Law, and were now "not God's people." (2) That the decree of Cyrus was a fulfilment of the prophecy of Jeremiah 29:1, in which it was promised that all the people whom Nebuchadezzar had taken away captive from Jerusalem into Babylon, should, after seventy years, be allowed to return. Now the House of Israel had not been carried away from Jerusalem by Nebuchadnezzar into Babylon. They had been taken from Samaria by the kings of Assyria, into Assyria ! (3) Nehemiah 11: 20: "And the residue of Israel of the priests, and the Levites,were in all the cities of Judah, every one in his inheritance." This could not include the Ten Tribes, as they had no inheritance in the cities of Judah. Their country was Samaria; now in possession of the strangers planted there by their Assyrian captors. (4.) When the children of Israel were building the temple, they were asked whence they came; they replied in effect that they had come from Babylon, thus giving denial to this theory, for the Ten Tribes had not been in Babylon. From all this it is evident that the theory of the Ten Tribes being absorbed by the Tribe of Judah is untenable. It is an attempt to adjust the Word of God to the theorists' conception of "natural sequences." No; if we want to trace the Ten Tribes, we must follow them "beyond the river," that is where God said they were to go.

CHAPTER XI.

In our last chapter we considered passages which, even taken by themselves, must refute the theory that the Israelites of the Northern Kingdom, or House of Israel, returned to Jerusalem with the Jews, when some of the latter (about 42.000) returned after seventy years captivity in Babylon. We have seen how it was expressly stated in 1 Chron. 5:26 (written after the end of the Babylonian captivity) that those of the Assyrian captivity were then in Assyria "unto this day." But, be it remembered, these passages are not the proofs of their non-return; they are just so much corroboration of that fact. The real proof is, that God had promised greatness, by His everlasting covenant. That promise is, to me at least, proof positive of the fact that their career did not end in miserable non-achieve- ment of any greatness. What though they brought upon themselves the punishment consequent on their idolatry, when they followed after, and departed not from the sins of Jeroboam the son of Nebat, who made Israel to sin, God's covenant with His "friend" Abraham could not be annulled by any sins of this people, in any generation, inasmuch as their conduct was no stipulation of the cove- nant, which, as we have seen, contained absolutely no condition whatever. The Oath of the Covenant was based on a "Because," twice repeated, but it contained no "If." (Read it, and see—Gen. 22: 16-18.) And so all passages pointed in confirmation of the covenant are merely to be taken as adjuncts, or as so much supplementary evidence. The covenant itself is the major premiss. The proof lies in the fact of the promise. "Hath He said· and shall He not make it good ?"

But the converse of this follows, as a matter of course; i.e. An interpretation of any passage of scripture whatever within the covers of the Bible, which deduces a failure, entirely or in part, of the promises conveyed by the everlasting covenant and oath of Jehovah, must necessarily and without fail be a wrong interpretation, leading to a wrong conclusion. What lapse of time; what devious ways notwithstanding; the course mapped out by God for His chosen people must be followed, and in His good time His people, scattered and divided though they have been, and still are, must converge to the point and climax of their destiny. Could this great truth grip the minds of our people, what an immensely more interesting and intelligible book of study, and of history, they would find the Bible to be. We should still, no doubt, continue to "see through a glass darkly." We should still have need of faith—the faith which made Abraham a "friend of God" —but if Abraham entered into the promises by faith, how much more ought we, whose faith is aided in a great measure by the evidence of things seen and enacted before our eyes. Yet the crying pity is that theologians (generally speaking) with all the advantages of education, and whose business it should be to study and correctly expound the Scriptures, so far from being insistent on the vindication of God's character of Truth, and the inevitability of the fulfilment of every last one of His promises (those of His promises which are plainly unconditional) they habitually take passages of Scripture, subsequent to these promises, and interpret them as nullifying verities already enacted, and even undertake to "justify" the non-fulfilment of promises (held to be unfulfilled, because not apprehended) by the explanation that sin entered in, and foiled the good purpose of God. As if sin was not already rampant on earth at the time the covenant was made, and as if God were unable to achieve His designs, despite the machinations of the author of sin

It is not for us to "explain" why God did not take a more direct way to accomplish His designs. Possibly, having endowed mankind with a Free Will, it was no part of His purpose to disendow them, and re-create automatons in place of men. He had displayed His wondrous work, and His gracious love to the Children of Israel; it was for them to make spontaneous response; a dictated worship would be valueless. Hence God left it to Jeroboam to commune in his heart, to do as his heart prompted him, and all Israel followed Jeroboam, of their own free will, into idolatry; hence the punishment which ensued. But even the form of punishment, the scattering and banishment of this people throughout long centuries was directed to- wards the end of a purpose unchanged.

But there is another theory; and that is, that the Ten Tribes, though they did not return, and become merged with the Jews, were not only dispersed amongst the Gentiles, but forever lost their status as God's people. Many passages are held to prove this—such as the follow- ing: "I will cause to cease the Kingdom of the House of Israel." "I will no more have mercy on the House of Israel, but will utterly take them away." These, and many other pronouncements against Israel in the period of their dispersion, are held to indicate that Israel of the Ten Tribes was utterly abandoned by God, and placed on a par with all other Gentile peoples for all time. Let me annihilate that theory in one word—the Covenant. What of it? How are you going to dispose of that rock? Oh, that is easily disposed of, in this wise—"The seed of Abra- ham are now to be regarded as a spiritual seed." But the promises were made to a literal seed, and if there is a statement in the Bible which says that God changed His mind, I have never come across it, nor seen it quoted. But I know of a passage which states that in God there is no

variableness, neither shadow of turning, and I conclude that
is literally true. All scripture testifies to that truth. I
find no passage to show that God abandoned His original
plan of choice of a certain people. The coming of Christ
did not alter this, for He told the Jews that the Kingdom
of God should be taken from them, and given unto a nation,
not to all and every nation. Nor can we spiritually interpret
the earthly predominance foretold for Ephraim and Manasseh, who were of the Ten Tribes, now scattered, but surely
wrongly held to be abandoned ! True they were commissioned with a spiritual mission, for in them should all
nations of the earth be blessed; and true, "whosoever will"
may be grafted in under the terms of the New Covenant,
and so enjoy the spiritual blessings, as well as partake of
the temporal blessings. But nowhere do we find that the
sons of Joseph were disinherited, or deposed from leadership amongst the nations of the earth. And so, looking
abroad on the world, we see the Anglo-Saxon race, British
and American, in the position of pre-eminence; from which
must follow the inevitable conclusion, that these must be
Ephraim and Manasseh, wonderfully placed in position, and
equipped with the requisite power to carry out God's
purpose. I do not conceive that this is a less inspiring
conclusion for men and women of our race to arrive at,
than that all mankind are now placed on a par, and that
God altered His original plan, and has now no chosen people,
and nothing more to do with earthly governments.

CHAPTER XII.

We have now come to a point in the history of God's chosen people, of the birthright House of Joseph, when they were divorced from Him, and scattered among the Gentile or heathen peoples in consequence of their sins. Many passages addressed to or relating to them in this temporary state of banishment have, for many hundreds of years, been misconstrued into meaning that they were utterly cast off for ever; with the rather vague reservation in most minds that, presumably after Christ's second coming, the "Jews" are to be rehabilitated in the land of Palestine, and in some such way the promises to Abraham are to be fulfilled. I have already amplified the fact that the Abrahamic covenant contains elements of prophecy which absolutely cannot be fulfilled in that way; although the eventual return of the Jews to Palestine, in a representative sense "One of a city, and two of a family" (Jer. 3:14) is a part of the prophecy, which is of course destined to be fulfilled; when " 'In those days' the house of Judah shall walk with (or to) the house of Israel, and they shall come together out of the land of the north, to the land that I have given for an inheritance unto your fathers" (Jer. 3:18). In reference to this text The Speaker's Commentary confirms the marginal reading—thus, Judah shall walk to Israel. And the same competent authority states that "In those days" is equivalent to "In the latter days."

Now the latter days are our days, and when we witness the Jews living with, or walking with, or walking to, the Anglo-Saxons: and see the land of Palestine in occupation of the British, who have driven out the Turks: bringing to an end "the times of the Gentiles" (Luke 21:24) and making arrangements for the rehabilitation of the Jews in

Jerusalem and Palestine—if we see all this, and much more, without realizing that the Anglo-Saxons must be the house of Israel, then we are either blind or indifferent, and we are paying scant heed to our Lord's words—Luke 12:54-57 —"How is it that ye do not discern this time ?" Facts are not altered by our failure to realize them, and the day may not be far distant when many will stand amazed at their own blindness. We are now passing through the most critical time in our nation's history, beset by enemies within and without, and there is nothing I think that can inspire courage and confidence more than a full realization that our race is under God's special care, destined to be preserved for His purpose. These are times when our people should make a determined effort to free their minds of inconsequential and passing considerations, whether of business or pleasure. No man should let his business or his pleasure get over his head. He should shake himself free of the shackles, and find time to interest himself in greater things than these.

Josephus, the Jewish historian, who wrote in A.D. 70, says "The Ten Tribes did not return to Palestine; only Two Tribes served the Romans after Palestine became a Roman province." And, again, "There are but Two Tribes in Asia and Europe subject to the Romans, while the Ten Tribes are beyond Euphrates till now, and are an immense multitude." This statement from history bears out the pronouncement of God, that the house of Jeroboam was to be scattered beyond the river. So that present-day theologians who strive to prove that the Ten Tribes were absorbed with the Jews, who were in subjection to the Romans in Palestine, have against them such authorities as Joesphus, writing in a comparatively contemporary period, and God Almighty, in His Divine capacity, speaking before the fact. How these authorities come to be ignored I know not; let us waste no further time with such a vain argument.

Now we shall consider some of the corroborations of the covenant, in passages addressed to the Israelites during their banishment, and see what indications there are to be found in the Bible itself that the Ten Tribes were eventually to make their way to the British Islands. It must be borne in mind that they were to be lost, which could only take place by their losing sight of their own identity; from which it of course follows that there could be no explicit statement in the Bible that they journeyed from Assyria to the British Islands; for in that case they would not be "lost tribes," uncovenanted, and under punishment for their sins; and in line for redemption under the New Covenant, according to God's plan.

The following are some of the promises, upbraidings, and pleadings addressed to Israel in banishment. "I will appoint a place for my people Israel, and will plant them, that they may dwell in a place of their own and move no more." "Where is the bill of your mother's divorcement, whom I have put away ? or which of my creditors is it to whom I have sold you ? Behold for your iniquities have ye sold yourselves, and for your transgressions is your mother put away." Yet, "Thou shalt break forth on the right hand and on the left; and thy seed shall inherit the Gentiles, and make the desolate cities to be inhabited." "Is Ephraim my dear son ? is he a pleasant child ? for since I spake against him I do earnestly remember him still." (This though Ephraim's mother, Israel, is temporarily put away.) "I will make a new covenant **with the house of Israel and with the house of Judah.**" (This indicates that God's chosen people of the **Twelve Tribes** are His first care even under the New Covenant. It also harmonizes with the historical fact that Israel came first under the covenant of Christianity. Judah is to follow in good time.) "Thou art my battle-axe and weapons of war: for with thee will I break in pieces the nations, and with thee will I destroy kingdoms." (This is a pre-millennial prophecy, of the "latter days," for after Christ's second coming there will be no more of battle-axes and war. We have just witnessed its partial fulfilment. Beyond all controversy Britain was the chief factor in the late war.) "I will bring you out from the people, and will gather you out from the countries wherein ye are scattered, with a mighty hand—and I will bring you into the wilderness of the people, and there will I plead with you face to face. And I will cause you to pass under the rod, and I will bring you under the bond of the covenant. And thou shalt take thine inheritance in thyself in the sight of the heathen." (They were to be a separate people; with the heathen, but not of the heathen.) "Plead with your mother, plead: for she is not my wife, neither am I her husband. She shall follow after her lovers, but she shall not overtake them; she shall seek them but shall not find them." (Woden-worship and Druidism would not satisfy this people.) "Then shall she say, I will go and return to my first husband, for then it was better with me than now." (This repentance was the purpose of their punishment.) "Therefore, behold, I will allure her, and bring her into the wilderness, and speak comfortably unto her." (Under the influence of these allurements **they must away!** They could not rest with the heathen or become lost in the Gentiles, they were always wandering and warring tribes.) "How shall I give thee up, Ephraim? How shall I deliver thee, Israel? Mine heart is turned within me, my repentings are kindled together." (How great is God's love for his chosen people!) "I will not execute the fierceness of mine anger, I will not return to destroy Ephraim: for I am God, and not man: the Holy One in the midst of thee." (These words are all addressed to Israel, not Judah; could we have more positive proof that Israel was not cut off, and that nothing is left of God's people but a scattered remnant of Judah?)

But why were they not allowed to rest ? Why not settle down in middle Europe, and there be restored to God's grace ? No; they were to be led to the best place; they must occupy the strategic position of the world. This was necessary since they were to become the "chief of the nations"; the "company of nations," and the "great people" of Ephraim and Manasseh. The covenant, in short, must be fulfilled. Now mark the following passages in Isaiah, all addressed to Israel of the Ten Tribes: "Hearken unto me, my people; and give ear unto me, O my nation . . . . . My righteousness is near . . . . . the Isles shall wait upon me, and on mine arm they shall trust." "Listen, O Isles, unto me; and hearken my people from far. Thou art my servant, O Israel, in whom I will be glorified." "They shall lift up their voice, they shall sing for the majesty of the Lord, they shall cry aloud from the sea. Wherefore glorify ye the Lord in the fires, even the name of the Lord God of Israel in the isles of the sea·" "Keep silence before me, O islands; and let the people renew their strength." "The isles shall wait for his law. Sing unto the Lord a new song, and his praise from the end of the earth." (The prayer book of the Church of England, the national church, bears blind testimony to all this. These are the themes of all the beautiful chants sung in the national church of the isles. The "Magnificat," the "Cantate," the "Nunc Dimittis," the "Jubilate" and the "Te Deum"; all lauding and praising God for His mercy, love, and deliverance—of whom ? "His servant Israel"—"Our forefathers, Abraham and his seed forever"—"Thy chosen people"—"Thy people"—"Thine inheritance"—"Thy heritage." But as yet, the testimony of the prayer book is not generally backed up in the pulpits. That, it is to be hoped, will not be long delayed; and meantime, be it noted, these prophecies are being fulfilled, for **the people are actually singing these songs in the isles,** even though they are not generally aware of their own identity). "Ye that go down to the sea, and all that is therein: the isles and the inhabitants thereof. Let them give glory unto the Lord, and declare His praise in the islands." (A maritime people is here indicated.)

These are not the rambling vagaries of a visionary, nor the platitudes of an essayist. It should be remembered they are the words of God Himself, through Isaiah, hence they cannot be meaningless. The isles are mentioned over and over again in Isaiah· What isles ? They lay to the north and west of Palestine. at the very "end of the earth" as then known. No other islands than the British islands lie in that direction. And no other islands on the face of the earth are inhabited by a great sea-going Christian people, who glorify God in songs of praise **for His good-ness to His people Israel.** It is a very strong case for the Islands !

CHAPTER XIII.

Something in the foregoing chapters aroused the ire
of a Methodist Minister, who wrote the first of the two
letters which will be found in "The Critics' Corner", at
the end of this book. My chapters, up to the 18th, constitute a series of articles written gratis for the press, at a
great deal of personal inconvenience. It will be understood that a man going before the public with such a
subject as this, cannot do so without using due care and
labour to get his data correct. This I had tried to do,
and thought I was telling an honest story; therefore I did
not see the propriety of a minister seeking to interrupt
and discredit a writer before he had finished his task.
Personally, I had never interrupted a minister, Methodist
or otherwise, in his discourse. Furthermore, I felt a rather
natural resentment at having the public told that British-
Israel exponents were engaged in perpetrating a "hoax".
I took that insult to myself—but not "lying down." My
other clerical adversary told the world that we were "foisting" a story on the Bible, and picking out texts here and
there to support fad theories. These plain accusations had
better be answered, perhaps, by a laconic negative; so, for
the information of the public generally, I will say that,
despite our Christian brethren to the contrary, we really
are not rogues—nor yet fools. I think I may make this
dogmatic assertion especially on behalf of the number of
bishops, clergy, and eminent scholars who are to be found
in the ranks of believers in this thesis. They are really
honest. Also "sane."

At this point it will be well for my reader to examine
carefully these pseudo-criticisms, and, putting yourself in
my place, you may be able to understand the resentment

which I am at no great pains to conceal. The following,
just as it appeared in the paper, was my reply to the first
critic —

I do not know whether I was glad or sorry to read
Mr. Puttenham's letter of the 2nd inst. in criticism of the
subject of these articles. I will turn it to the best advantage I can by allowing this week's instalment to partake
of the nature of a reply. I would have welcomed fair
criticism, and I respect the opinions of others, but I demur
at criticism, which has more than a suspicion of browbeating
and a large measure of contempt. Such criticism I would
not answer were it concerning myself alone, but having
brought this matter before the reading public, I feel bound
to do it the justice of defending it, lest readers may get
the impression that it is only a "theory" held by certain
ill-informed persons, and not entertained by "scholars."

My best course, then, will be to cite a few of the names
of those who, according to the "scholarly pen" of the high
placed "American scholar" endorsed by my critic, are
guilty of a "stratagem" and engaged in perpetrating a
"hoax," with the mere object of flattering the English
and Americans. I take the names haphazard from a book
before me · The Rt. Rev. J. C. Ryle, Lord Bishop of Liver-
pool; Rt. Rev. Bishop Titcomb; Rev. Mark Guy Pearse;
Ven. Archdeacon Hanan, M.A., D.D.; Dean Stanley; the
Rector of Sunk Island; Rev. W. M. H. Milner, "Oxonian",
and a host of others, of whom these are typical. It would
ill-become me to forget that doughty Britisher, my fellow
Irish countryman, Dr. Patterson, of Cooke's Presbyterian
Church, Toronto, from whom I heard the first of this subject. (I hope he has read some of my articles, to show
him how close attention I paid to his two hours' eloquent
lecture here in Ottawa a few years ago.) At the First
Annual British-Israel World Federation Congress, held in
London last July, those who took part included two bishops

of the Established Church of England, one bishop of the
Wesleyan Methodist Church of the United States, the
Bishop of the Falkland Islands, an ex-President of the
English Wesleyan Conference, many clergymen of the
Anglican Church, and ministers of the Congregational,
Wesleyan and Baptist Churches of the British Empire and
the United States. And amongst the laymen, members of
the House of Lords, the army and the navy, the medical,
legal, and other professions, university men and leading
merchants, H.R.H. Princess Alice, Dr. Rice Oxley, Mayor
of Kensington, etc., etc. The delegates attending were
from such widely separated parts of the Empire as New
Zealand, Australia, and Canada. Did they come these
great distances for the sake of flattering each other ?

Is it, I wonder, the contention that these people are
not as "scholarly" as the writer of the specimen of English
literature quoted by my critic ? I will leave it to readers
to say if it is probable that these people are concerned
about publishing "twaddle and nonsense"—"all a stratagem and a hoax to flatter the English and Americans, for
those nations have a superfluity of egotism and pomposity"?
That is the scholarly statement, which my critic says shows
the other side! I don't say it shows the other side, but my
critic does. I hope I have more respect for the opinion of
the other side than to say this represents it. I have no
time to waste on a man who has so little respect for the
honest opinion of others. It may be scholarly, but it sounds
foolish to me. Talking about egotism and pomposity—
the shoe is on the other foot. "A Mr. Byers" would remind
"the Mr. Puttenham" that after all there may be "more
things in heaven and earth than are dreamed of in his
philosophy." I have studied too much, and listened too
long to others who had studied, to be carried away by
the brusque dictum that "the secret of Great Britain's
greatness is not in any relation, for there is none, to the

Jew, but **because** Great Britain in the 16th century covenanted never to have any association with the man of sin,
the Pope." (I prefer to find the secret in the **because** of
God's Covenant in Gen. 22:16, 18) I was not aware that
Great Britain covenanted never to have any association
with the Pope, but if that is the fact it is a pity she broke
her covenant; she has an envoy at the Vatican at the present time. Is it not so? My critic's letter was headed
"Anglo-Israelism, a Dangerous Delusion," but I did not
fail to notice that he omitted to point out the danger, in
fact, he does not mention the word "danger" at all. As
to its being a delusion, that is an opinion, a bare statement
of opinion unsupported by any argument. Here is another
opinion: I have for some time held the opinion that it is a
"delusion" to suppose that clergy of the Roman Catholic
Church are the only ones who arrogate to themselves the
interpretation of the Bible.

I could quote a lot of very dry reading comprising the
findings of students who have compared the works of
Sharon Turner, the historian of the Anglo-Saxons; M. Paul
de Chaillu, the Frenchman; Herodotus, and many others,
in proof that the Anglo-Saxons are of Semitic and not of
Japhetic origin, and that the "Scyths" or wanderers, who
are shown by the Greek historian, Herodotus, to have **"en
tered Europe at the very epoch by the self-same route, and
from the identical district in Asia, at, by, and from which
journeyed the Israelites of Esdras,"** are identical with the
"Scots" who made their way to Ireland, and thence to
Scotland. (My quotation is from "British-Israel Truth.")
However, I thought it better to present the subject in a
more generally readable form, leaving the technicalities of
ethnology to the last; and in the long series of articles
which I am writing I have given simple reasons and explanations at every step, carefully avoiding dogmatisms.
I submit that I have not been trying to "hoax" anybody.

Readers are invited to draw their own conclusions from the
fact that God made certain clearly-defined covenant promises of place and position to the seed of Abraham, that
those places and that position are now held by the Anglo-
Saxons, British and American, which I think makes it
plain that these nations are those to whom the promises
were made; ergo, these nations are the seed of Abraham,
of the birthright House of Joseph; not Jews but Israelites.
Hence, of course, there is a relation to the Jews; also, since
the Jews are of Semitic origin, the Anglo-Saxons are of
Semitic origin. That is the position, and this is a reasoned
denial of my critic's unsupported statement to the contrary. Any other conclusion would involve the argument
that promises made to one people could be "fulfilled" to
another, which is absurd. The promises are either kept
or broken; take your choice. If I promise anything to one
man, and give it to someone else (not even a relation of
his), I suppose it would be fair to say, I break my promise.
This is only kindergarten logic. If the promise was a
conveyance of land, or something valuable, secured by
covenant oath in legal form, I would be sued for breach
of contract. This is the logic of the law. Is the logic of
theology different? If it is, you could hardly blame a
business-man for falling asleep during the sermon. In a
recent article I said the Covenant is the major premiss—
meaning that we are basing our argument on that foundation; which renders it unnecessary for readers to study
Herodotus or Sharon Turner, unless they have the time and
the patience to do so. Most people hardly find time to
read their Bible: in any case, I would recommend them to
study that first. But readers are free to take their choice
between this style of argument and that of my critic. No
doubt some will agree with his dictum that "of relation
to the Jew there is none," but I don't think very many will
fall in with the none too well-bred assertion that it is all

"twaddle and nonsense." Suppose we don't all agree with the "scholarly American," what then ? Some do and some don't. We are not taking anybody's dictation

When Mr. Puttenham procures his ammunition I will be glad to hear more of "the other side." I have read a good deal of the other side, but nothing quite as crude as the extract he quoted. I may say, I had the pleasure of hearing Dr. Baron in the Old Country (though not on this subject) in a lecture, which was an intellectual treat His book, "The History of the Lost Tribes," however, was refuted in a work by Landseer MacKenzie I have been told that the Orangeman, Professor Odlum, of Vancouver, started into the study with the idea of disproving the "theory," and finished up as one of its strongest supporters. I have read his book, "God's Covenant Man," which specially appealed to me, as it was the most determined book on the subject of all that I have read. As I have received numerous letters of keen appreciation from places as far apart as Regina, Boston, and Washington, etc., I will try to continue the rather difficult task of compiling a readable account out of a mass of rather dry technical matter which I am studying from. It must be borne in mind that after the Assyrian captivity the Israelites were "lured away" to the wilderness, and there is no further historical account of them in the Bible, hence a narrative of their further travels must look to secular history and a comparison of legends. It is obvious that if the Bible, or any ancient history book, contained a precise statement that they went direct to the British Islands they would never have been lost ! Also. as the **dispersion was a punishment for their sins,** as well as a preparation for the broad future in which the seed of Abraham was to expand to all nations and climes, it is not surprising that they were very much lost, and not easy to trace.

Here the question may arise. If God chose to lead them

away, and caused them to lose consciousness of their identity, why should we try to find them ? That is a reasonable
question. The answer is, I believe, that they were to be
found again, and the process of finding has been in operation for a number of years. Students of prophecy, com-
paring the symbolical "times" and "weeks" of the prophet
Daniel with the trend of events relating to Palestine, were
of the opinion that the "times of the Gentiles" would have
been fulfilled when Jerusalem had ceased to be "trodden
down of the Gentiles," after which Judah and Israel were
to be reunited in Jerusalem and Palestine. This conclusion
is arrived at in a book, written before the great war, which
I have before me. The Turks have been driven out of
Jerusalem, and driven out by the British alone, in accordance with prophecy, hence, as we are now in the "latter
days," the study is strictly proper, unless it can be main-
tained that we should pay no heed to Biblical prophecies
at all. Is that, I wonder, the contention ?

I shall take no further notice of interruptions until I
have finished. Afterwards, if invited to do so, I will be
only too pleased to join in any fairly conducted discussion
(with Mr. Puttenham or anyone else) to which the columns
of The Sentinel may be open; but I will not interfere with
his presentation of his views when he gets Dr. Baron's
book. Let someone else take it up. There is a British-
Israel branch in Toronto, and writers, I am sure, better
equipped with books of reference than I am. I would
like to add that I opened this subject in The Sentinel on
set purpose. I think it would be a most fitting topic of
discussion for Orange lodges. Knowledge is power. You
have the "Open Bible." Read it, you Britishers, and discover therein that the enemy you most dread shall not
triumph against the Covenant-People !

CHAPTER XIV.

We have taken only a brief glance at some of the many passages which mark the location of the **interim home** or gathering point of the scattered ten tribes, that sea-girt, impregnable home, that "place of their own," from which they were to "move no more" against their will, that "goodly land" beside the "great waters," where the vine could take root, whose branches were to spread and fill the face of the world with fruit (Isaiah 27 6) It was the trumpet of God which sounded the "Assembly," and the **Isles** were well chosen as a safe rallying point for the scattered but imperious fugitives, who fought their way home and would not be denied entry to its haven. "Keep silence before me, O Islands; and let the people renew their strength" (Isa. 41:1). Who are the people who were to renew their strength in silence during long centuries in the Islands—renew their strength until the strength of the race has reached an immensity and a volume without parallel; the strength of Ephraim and Manasseh united, whose might is yet unknown, for the time is yet in the future when they, united, shall "push the people together to the ends of the earth"—"the ten thousands of Ephraim and the thousands of Manasseh"—the strength, in short, which is to justify such a prophecy—who are these people, in "the islands"? Read on and see in the 8th verse, "Thou, Israel art my servant, Jacob, whom I have chosen, the seed of Abraham my friend"—"Thou are my servant; I have **chosen thee and not cast thee away.**"

What? After all! Not cast away, up to the time when they had reached the islands, and subsequent to their divorce from the Mosiac covenant ! No, not cast away up to then, nor since, nor ever. An everlasting covenant, as I understand it, is a covenant that has no ending.

It is a pity that one cannot dwell on all the finger-posts of Scripture which point to the islands; volumes might be written on these alone; I can only notice a few of them. The passage in Isaiah 49:12 is very definite as to direction; it refers to the, still in the future, restoration of Zion, when "Behold these (the restored ones) shall come from far: and lo, these from the North and from the West." The chapter opens with, "Listen, O Isles, unto me: and hearken, ye people from far." There is no compound word in the Hebrew for North-West, but the expression "North and West" is sufficiently explicit to identify the Islands home of the Israelites as the British Islands, for they are the only islands of any size North-West from Palestine. It is a pity that people read Bible passages as if they were rambling or random statements. There is no part of the world now undiscovered, and we don't look to China and the Orient for the "great nation" and "company of nations" which, we have God's word for it, were to "inherit the desolate heritages," and carry blessing to "all nations." Neither do we assume that, in spite of all the great predictions about them, the ground opened and swallowed them up. No, we look for an existing "great nation" and "company of nations," as we are bound to do, since they were "established" by an "everlasting covenant," and we see them in the place where all the prophecies said they would be. The covenant would not have been fulfilled had God's people developed into the heathen Chinese, or been engulfed by an earthquake. That is plain.

What, then, is the position of those who refuse to recognize the origin and identity of the race which occupies the place foretold for the seed of Abraham? It is in the main a position of indifference, or worse. Hardly any will say point-blank that God broke His covenant: but, how do they get around it? What we need nowadays is intellectual honesty, coupled with knowledge. Paine, the atheist, was, perhaps, intellectually honest; he based his atheism largely on the misconception that God's promises to "the Jews" had not been kept; and it was ignorance rather than intellectual dishonesty that made him an infidel. He might not have turned atheist had he possessed the simple knowledge that the promises were not made to "the Jews," but to the father of the Hebrew race, comprising two distinct nations, Jews and Israelites. All "Jews" are, of course, Israelites, or children of Israel, but, roughly speaking, eleven-twelfths of the children of Israel are not Jews, they are simply Israelites. This need not be confusing to anyone who has no difficulty in understanding so obvious a statement as, for instance, that all Englishmen are British, but all British are not English. There is not much of a puzzle about that. Yet so puzzled are the majority of our people that, not seeing the promises fulfilled to the Jews, they jump to the conclusion that the word "Israel" must mean a Gentile church, and a "spiritual seed," not a seed that was to proceed out of Abraham's loins, to whom the promises were made, and this satisfies them, although it entails the argument that a promise given to one people can be "fulfilled" to someone else, which is absurd. It did not satisfy Paine, apparently, for he concluded that the promises were all a myth. One can hardly be intellectually honest along those lines.

For the benefit of all genuine seekers for knowledge, God fully explains the reason of His rough-handling of the children of Israel. In Ezekiel 22: 15, we read, "I will scatter thee among the heathen and disperse thee in the countries"—and utterly consume thee ? Oh, no ! He doesn't say that; what He says is, "**and will consume thy filthiness out of thee.**" Let this dispose of the theory that they were utterly destroyed; if that were to happen, it would hardly be worth-while to consume their filthiness out of them first. Dead men cannot worship God. Their "filthiness" we may, I think, assume to be their idolatry; and that this was consumed out of them harmonizes with the prediction that "they that escape of you shall remember Me among the nations whither they shall be carried." "They shall lift up their voice, they shall sing for the majesty of the Lord, they shall cry aloud from the sea"; as well as harmonizing with their ultimate destiny to be a blessing to all nations. Why not pursue the study of the fortunes of this people with a view to tracing out how the promises have been fulfilled, instead of assuming that it was impossible for God to retain such a wicked people in His favor, and engaging in the hardly inspiring task of explaining away the failure? Is the task too difficult? Well, for my part, it would be much more difficult to explain the failure; that, at least, is impossible; I couldn't do it, and be intellectually honest. Of course, the task is difficult; all study is difficult, and the study of a history which is **largely unwritten** has its special difficulties. But we should remember that "It is the glory of God to conceal a thing; but the honour of kings to search out a matter." Certainly it should be to the honour of anyone to search out a matter like this, which aims at the vindication of the Truth of the whole Word of God; and those of us who firmly believe that that Word concerns our own race, find it a delightful study; doubly important in that it concerns our present and future, as well as our past.

But, to get on with our narrative. We read in the book of Esdras, "The Ten Tribes were carried prisoner out of their own land in the time of Osea, the king whom Shalmanezer, the king of Assyria, led away captive, and he carried them over the waters, and so they came into another land. But they took counsel among themselves that they would leave the multitude of the heathen and go forth into a further country where never mankind dwelt.

And they entered into Euphrates by the narrow passage
of the river. For through that country was a great way
to go—namely, of a year and a half—**and the same region
is called Arsareth.**'' Josephus confirms this movement, as
we have seen, when he states, ''The entire body of the Ten
Tribes are still beyond Euphrates, an immense multitude
not to be estimated by numbers.'' Ancient historians refer
to a people who appeared in this region at that time, and
who were known, variously, as the Getæ, the Massagetæ,
and by the general name of ''Scuths'' or ''Scythians,''
signifying ''Wanderers''—which bears out the prophecy,
''They shall be Wanderers among the nations.'' They were
not indigenous to that region; for Herodotus declares,
''They were the most recent of nations, having existed only
for a thousand years.'' This would place the date of their
origin at about the time of the Exodus from Egypt.
Æschylus refers to them as ''Scythians, governed by good
laws.'' Homer says they were the most just of men, ''the
justest of mankind.'' Evidently, these remarkable Wanderers were under the influence of traditional if unwritten
laws. The long previously delivered law of Moses ? John
Milton refers to the Saxons as ''a people descended from the
Scythians of Sacai, afterwards called Sacasons, who, with
a flood of other nations, came into Europe about the time
of the decline of the Roman Empire.'' M. de Chaillu, in
''The Viking Age,'' asserts that ''the **ancestors of the English came from the Black Sea.**'' Which is the same region
as the Arsareth of Esdras, and the Cimmerian Bosphorous
or Crimea. Many tombstones have been discovered in this
region bearing inscriptions in Hebrew. Herodotus says of
the Sacæ in the Persian armies, ''The Sacæ, who are Scythians, wore caps which came to a point at the top, and stood
erect.'' The same pointed caps were found later on in
ornaments on Scythian tombs on the banks of the Dneiper,
where they passed in their slow travel toward the ''North

and West.'' Khumri or Kymri was the name given on
Assyrian tablets to Samaria, the capital city of Israel.
This name is perpetuated in Wales, for the Welsh people
were otherwise known as Cymru or Cymri, and the ancient
name of that part of Britain was Cambria.   Other
names by which the Scythians were known in Europe
are the Belgæ, Goths, Ostro-Goths, Dacians, Milesians,
Danes, Jutes, Angles, Saxons, Normans, or Northmen; who
all at different periods found their way to the British Islands, coming from different directions, as was natural for
scattered wanderers to come, and finally merging into one
people, which would not be quite so natural did they not
eventually recognize, when they stopped fighting long
enough to compare notes, that they all originally evidently
came of the same stock, having many traditions and tenden-
cies in common. Unfortunately the Phœnicians also came;
these are now known as Fenians, or rather, their latest name
is Sinn Fein, and, bear witness all, these are not of the same
stock as the other British Islanders. Canaanites they are,
and they are not of the number of Israel. It is believed
that the Khumri were amongst the first to arrive in Wales.
But by far the most interesting part of our story centres
around the Tribe of Dan, the Tuatha da Danaan of
ancient Irish history. These are not to be confused with
the Phœnician-Irish.   They probably were the first to
arrive, in the North of Ireland, hundreds of years before
the other Britons. Why they should have come so much
earlier may readily be understood when we remember the
little text which tells that ''Dan abode in ships.'' This
was the mariner tribe of ancient Israel: they naturally took
to their ships when they left for foreign parts, and travellers
by ship cannot settle down anywhere en route. A good
deal of our story hinges on this tribe, as we shall see.

CHAPTER XV.

It is the tribe of Dan which furnishes most of the concrete data from which the story of Israel, after its disappearance from Biblical history, is pieced out. It is this tribe at least that supplies the connecting links to bridge over the chasm between a great nation which has disappeared out of the Bible, and a great nation that has taken shape in the modern world strictly in conformity with the Scriptural predictions relating to the very nation which has disappeared, that is to the House of Israel of the lost ten tribes, including Dan in its number. In order, then, to at all clearly understand on what grounds, apart from faith in the Covenant, the belief is based that the children of the birthright House found their way to the British Islands, it is very important that we should take particular note of the geographical situation, as well as some of the tribal characteristics of this tribe.

In Josh. 19 : 47, we read that "The coast of the children of Dan went out too little for them; therefore the children of Dan went up to fight against Leshem, and took it and possessed it and dwelt therein, and called Leshem Dan after the name of Dan, their father." Again (in Judges 18: 11, 12) some of them "went up and pitched in Kirjath-jearim, in Judah, **wherefore** they called that place Mahaneh-dan unto this day." We are not told that they possessed this place; they merely pitched their tents and in the next verse "they passed thence." Yet again they came to Laish and took that; "and they called the name of the city Dan, after the name of Dan, their father, who was born unto Israel; howbeit the city was Laish at the first." Now I want to make three points out of all this. The first is that the children of Dan were evidently not ashamed of their name; they were an adventurous people: they had, or I am assuming it likely they had, a roving disposition, coupled with a predilection for seizing places attractive to them; but whether they intended to permanently possess these places or merely to pitch their passing tents, their propensity was **to call the places after Dan, the father of their tribe.** This naming of places was, in any case, a Hebrew custom, while with Dan it was a tribal habit to brand places with their own name: call it esprit de corps, or plain covetousness—what you will—but the important fact remains that a tribe doing this would necessarily leave their trail behind them wherever they went. Nor is it unreasonable to suppose that Dan was not imbued with this instinct by chance. In Jer. 31:21, the command is given: "Set thee up waymarks . . . . . even the way which thou wentest: turn again, O virgin of Israel, turn again to these thy cities." What would be the purpose of these waymarks ? So that God could trace them ? Hardly. The only purpose that I can see would be that they might be able to retrace their steps, or, in other words, rediscover their own identity in the "latter days" when the time had come for them to "turn again." But, again, of what use would waymarks be if we did not know their import ? My second point is, that the fully detailed account of the otherwise to us unimportant early adventures of Dan is expressly given as an **index to the waymarks.** We are told that the Scriptures are written for our learning. Very well, we learn from these Scriptures that where we find the name of Dan we are to conclude that Dan passed that way.

Supposing these assumptions to be correct, and that the authorities already quoted are correct in assuming that the ten tribes escaping from the Assyrian captivity, entered Europe by the Caucasian Pass and travelled thence by very slow degrees across the European continent, possessing lands and dwelling in them for various periods as they tended, rather than travelled, toward the "north and west," then it would be natural to look for some traces of the tribe of Dan, the track-leaving tribe. And here we are not disappointed, for Dan has blazed his trail very industriously along the line of route; and, like Mahaneh-dan, the names have stuck "to this day." The name is not always simply "Dan"; Mahaneh-dan is a Scripturally authentic example of the variations. It will also be well here to mention that in the ancient Hebrew there were no **written** vowels, so that Dan was written simply "D-N," the vowel sound taking the form of the particular dialect of the speaker; so that a change of the word to Don, Din, or Dun, or the omission of the vowel altogether, would not be sufficient to bar the evidence. Well, what do we find ? The Don, the Danube, the Danastris (now Dneister), the Danapris (now Dneiper), which rivers they would cross, or along whose course they would follow, and where Dan would leave his trail, on up through Europe till we come to Denmark,or Danemerke,as the old name was(literally Dan's mark), in which country, by the way, about three hundred years ago, a Danish peasant girl, plowing in a field, turned up with her plow a golden trumpet, now in the National Museum at Copenhagen, and identified beyond all doubt as one of the seven trumpets used in the altar service at Jerusalem. The tribes evidently passed that way, and Dan apparently went overland along with the other tribes, leaving his "waymarks" en route.

Now we come to the third point, and this is extremely important in the line of study we are taking. Let us look back at the text, "The coast of the children of Dan went out too little for them." So the children of Dan—that is, some of them, as the Bible account shows—went up to fight against Leshem, and so on. But part of them remained behind, still retaining possession of their coast settlement; they were not giving up anything; they were simply out for more possessions. Thus we have two Danish colonies—one on the coast and one inland. At the back of my Bible I find a map (we don't often look at these maps) it shows the land of Canaan as divided among the tribes, and I see that Dan held a small section on the coast of the Mediterranean, south of the lot of Ephraim, and shut off on the east by Benjamin. (These boundaries are significant, as we shall note later on.) This was the coast territory of Dan, which they found too small; it had Joppa for a seaport. Thus situated, it is not surprising to find that Dan was a seafarer. As early as 1296 B.C. we find, in the song of Deborah, that Dan is taunted with remaining in his ships while the other tribes fought off the inland invaders, Jabin and Sisera. (Judges 5:17.) The reason of Dan's delinquency is, perhaps, irrelevant; it could hardly be cowardice, as this was a fighting tribe; possibly it was a case of temperament, or tribal pique or jealousy. Quite possibly it was no part of God's plan that Dan should be drawn away from his ships to go inland; he was needed elsewhere.

But the important point to notice is that Dan was a sailor. We know that King Solomon possessed a navy as early as about a thousand years before Christ, with ships coming from Tarshish every three years. I. Kings 10:22. (Tarshish must have been a long way off.) Again, Jonah went to Joppa, the seaport of Dan, and took passage in a ship going to Tarshish, and **"paid the fare thereof"**—even as you or I—there's nothing new under the sun! If this "paying the fare thereof" has any significance, it means that Tarshish was somewhere beyond the seas, with a passenger and freight traffic fully established between it and Palestine, as early as 860 years before Christ. Hard to believe, is it? Well, there is the Bible account. (Jonah 1:3.) This trade was carried on with Tarshish 300 years before the Assyrian captivity. Now in Isaiah 23:2, 6-7, we read: "Be still, **ye inhabitants of the isle; thou whom the merchants of Zidon that pass over the sea have replenished"**

. . . . "Pass ye over to Tarshish; howl ye inhabitants of the isle. Is this (Tyre) your joyous city, whose antiquity is of ancient days ?" Tyre and Zidon (or Sidon) were cities of Phœnicia. Phœnicia lay on the coast, just north of the coast of Dan. The Phoenicians peopled Ireland; that is authentic history. Now, where is Tarshish ? It is not on any map, for the reason, I believe, that the word does not signify any particular country. The phrase "to go to Tarshish" was, I believe, an idiomatic term, having the same elastic application as our own phrase "to go over-seas." When we use the word "oversea," in conversation, we always use it in reference to some particular settled country, which is understood by the person addressed to be the country referred to. But we do not use the term "overseas" in reference to a voyage of discovery, say to the North Pole; we call that "going on an expedition." Tarshish in this sense, then, would be a reference to some settled place that was understood in the conversation. Some writers take it to mean literally "the ends of the earth"; that is either end, from Palestine, which was at the Mediterranean, or middle of the earth. as then charted; and its general application in this sense would also be correct. It would mean the end of the earth either way, as was understood. We could hardly, for instance, sustain a theory that Solomon's ships bringing apes and peacocks from Tarshish, brought them from the **Northwest** Tarshish, or end of the earth. But this would not fix Tarshish in the South; for we know that the people of India, which has the apes and peacocks, could not be referred to as possessing the ships of Tarshish, which we shall refer to presently. "Tarshish" then would mean "overseas" in either direction; but it is with the Tarshish of the North-west that we are concerned, for the prophecies and the waymarks of Dan lead that way. Where, then, is this **particular Isle of Tarshish**, which was replenished by the merchants of Tyre, and peopled by the Phœnicians, from pre-historic days? Consult a map of the ancient world, and it will be seen that it is the island of Ireland which lies at the extreme North-west end of the earth. And **this** Tarshish includes the British Islands; a trading people is indicated, characterized by their possession of a great mercantile marine, dwellers, withal, on islands, answering to such descriptions as are contained in the following: "Sing with gladness for Jacob, and shout for the chief of the nations . . . . . . I will bring them from the **north** coun-try, and gather them from the uttermost parts of the earth." . . . . . . "Hear the Word of the Lord, O ye nations, and declare it in the **isles afar off**; and say, He that scat-tered Israel will gather him, and keep him." "Lo these shall come from the North and West." "Who are these that fly as a cloud, and as doves to their windows ? Surely the isles shall wait for me, and the ships of Tarshish first, to bring thy sons from far, their silver and their gold with them." (Re-establishing Palestine.)

Again, in Ezekiel 38:9, 12, 13, there is a prediction relating to the invasion of the Holy Land, after the reunion there of Israel and Judah. The invader will be the mys-terious Gog, the Prince of Rosh (possibly Russia), and we find he is to be opposed by men from Tarshish. "**The merchants of Tarshish, with all the young lions thereof,** shall say unto thee (Gog), Art thou come to take a spoil ?" Now, who are we to suppose that the defenders of Palestine may be, if not its recent deliverers and present protectors, the British ? The descriptions are most pointed. Napoleon once called us a nation of shopkeepers; he wasn't far out, though he discovered that we could be soldiers on occasion. The merchants of Tarshish and the young lions thereof is apparently a veiled name for Great Britain and her company of young nations; also the Americans. Oh, I'm not making any dogmatic statements, but—think it over.

CHAPTER XVI.

It is recorded in the Milesian annals of Ireland that Eochaid the Heremonn, or "Crowned Horseman," was a prince of the Tuatha da Danaan. We have not yet come to the point at which we will have to deal specially with this prince; but readers not already acquainted with the facts of history connected with this personage will do well to bear the name in mind. At this stage, suffice it to notice that Irish legendary history is specially rich in folk-lore, concerning the Tuatha da Danaan, rather than the Phœnician tribes, to which they were clearly superior. Now it is a curious fact that those Irish who are most prone to dwell loudly and long on the "days of Ireland's ancient glory" are the descendants of the very people who had the least to do with Ireland's ancient glory. And the tale of Ireland's glory is no myth; it may not be possible to say exactly at what period legend merges into history, but we know that it is recorded in the pages of authentic history that Ireland was at one time the seat of learning and Christianity—"The Lamp of Western Europe." But it is not generally known, or rather, it is generally forgotten that the ancient glory of Ireland was all anterior to the much more modern Roman Catholic religion: when that Church got the supremacy in Ireland her lamp began to burn very low. Well might the Harp of Tara hang mute, with only a breaking chord to tell to the stillness of the night the tale of her ruin. Tara ! Ah, well, Rome had no part in Tara. We shall have something more to say about Tara anon.

Biblical accounts already examined indicate unmistakably that the Isles of the North-west were replenished by the merchants of Tyre and Palestine. The Irish them-selves—not the pro-British Irish—stoutly maintain their descent from a people as ancient as the Phœnicians They claim a very ancient lineage; and with justice, though the conclusion we must draw from their grand claim is not as highly desirable as some of their biased historians would lead us to believe. The history of Ireland is perhaps the most puzzling in the world; inasmuch as that country bursts out into the arena of history with a civilization and gov-ernment (or governments, for there were several) already established, whose origin cannot be definitely accounted for except by inference. It is not my intention to branch off into the "Irish Question"; but let us note in passing that their claim to be the most ancient "nation" in Europe, except Greece, is badly handicapped by a number of facts, one of which is that the Irish, as such, have never yet been under one government.

Dr. McDonald, Roman Catholic Priest and Professor of Theology, Maynooth, in his masterful book, "Some Ethical Questions of Peace and War," lays down that—granting two essentials as conditional to nationhood, (1) Unity of Rule, and (2) Complete Independence—Ireland has never had a claim to nationhood, inasmuch as the Irish have always been lacking in one or other of these essential re-quirements. They never had Unity of Rule previous to coming into union with Great Britain. This gave them Unity of Rule, but necessarily barred the other essential, i.e., Complete Independence. The Irish, however, base their claim on such grounds as Unity of Race, Religion, and Natural Boundaries Unity of race and religion is not an essential, nor its lack a bar, to nationhood; as witness the United States of America, comprised of many races and creeds, yet a great nation And as for Natural Boundaries! The British Islands are naturally surrounded by the sea.

which gives them a splendid isolation and security from Europe. Since Great Britain has become a world power, she has recognized the importance of preserving this natural boundary intact. The Irish are claiming the right to set up an independent republic, under their pseudo president, one De Valera, a Spanish American, now masquerading in the United States as President of a mythical Irish republic. Will that independence be achieved ? I think not. It would at once cancel the efficiency of the British navy. It would destroy the position of Great Britain as the keystone of a world-wide Empire, causing the whole structure to fall apart. It would mean, in short, that the Empire would exist on sufferance, during the good-will of the Irish, and no longer. Such a shifty foundation of existence does not appeal to British intelligence.

But, has Ireland ever had Unity of Race ? Never ! It is a fact too often forgotten that there have been at least two distinct races of Irish people in Ireland from the earliest times. The Irish of the Tuatha da Danaan have at least as good a title in the country as their Phoenician compatriots. I have no patience with the North of Ireland Protestant Irishman who boasts that he is of Scottish descent. Does he not know that the Scotch are of North Irish descent, and that both are of "Scythian" descent ?

I have referred to the high-sounding claim of the anti-British Irish, that they are one of the most ancient races in Europe; and I have hinted that the conclusion is not as highly desirable as they would have us think. Granted that they are a very ancient race of people; where do they come from ? "Howl, ye inhabitants of the isle (singular). Is this (Tyre) your joyous city of ancient days ?" Yes, if it is their ancient lineage they are howling about, let them howl. They have declared themselves to be the most implacable and inveterate enemies of the British, and especially the English people; and they are at the present time engaged in backing up their declared sentiments by a long-drawn series of the most heinous murders that has fouled the history of any race of savages. We recognize them fully, and we recognize their earnestness. They are Phoenicians of the Palestinian country of Phœnicia. But the Tuatha da Danaan, from the adjacent territory, came at least as early to Ireland, and they will stay as long. I don't look for the disruption of the British Empire until I see a flaw in the Covenant upon which it is established. Don't I believe in Majority Rule ? Certainly I do. That is what we have in the British Islands. Do I believe in Self-Determination ? No, I don't. I believe in Majority Rule. You can't have it both ways.

"Self-Determination" ? What are its boundary lines ? Carried to its conclusion—or should one say, tracked to its lair ?—it is, finally, the snarl of the cave man. An American with any practical appreciation of the history of his own country should be the last to talk about self-determination. The greatest American president, one of the world's greatest men, gave his everlasting decision against it, as demanded by, say, Maryland. Lincoln, however, had one advantage; it was presented to him, practical end to, by the citizens of Baltimore. He had a good chance to see what it was, so he met it with a sword. New Englanders shouldered their muskets on Boston Common, to settle the question of government for the people of Virginia and Kentucky —without "the consent of the governed". Nobody hated oppression more than Abraham Lincoln did; rather, so much did he love liberty, that he refused to allow it to be broken into fragments by the secessionists. Statesmanlike, Lincoln kept liberty in bulk for "these united states". British statesmen are bound to perform the same duty for the British Empire. There is an advantage in seeing things from the practical end first. Yet an abstract-minded phrase was passed on, as a help, in the solution of European disputes. It was conceived in good faith, and launched with apparently no misgivings as to its practical effect when thrown into contact with the human element. It was not intended for Ireland, but that is where it arrived. The sole relict of the high sounding fallacy is, I believe, the "Self-Determination League for Ireland". It was snatched up by Irish-American agitators, as a lever to pry apart the armour of the British Empire; and now the abstract-minded phrase has become a practical factor in John Bull's Budget. It figures quite largely in his estimates for defence of the realm. John has to pay. Unhyphenated Americans regret it almost as much as the British. In justice to Mr. Wilson it should be said that if the Sinn Fein did not have his phrase to cite in support of their misdeeds, they would have something else. But meantime, the world is not so young and so green as to need a schoolmaster's phrase for a cue. We are out of kindergarten. The proved form of civilized government is Majority rule, with due respect for the rights of Minorities. The British Islands are a geographical unit. This the form of government which belongs to that part of the world.

Just recently I saw in the newspapers a condensed report of a sermon preached by a Canadian Anglican clergyman, stating his reasons for concluding that the United Kingdom was to be broken up, Ireland to be independent, and this to be followed by the general disintegration of the whole Empire. Such a man is decidedly welcome to his views; but I defy him to preach that sermon from a Bible passage. He might preach it from a Hearst newspaper. A little while ago I sat (not very patiently) under a preacher who, after declaring that he was a loyal British subject, and "as good an Orangeman as any" (though he wasn't an Orangeman at all !) went on to state that Ireland was to have separation from the British Empire and— Oh, he was sorry for it ! but he was bound to declare it—

the British Empire was to come to an end. Why ? Because
the Bible said so ! The Jews were God's chosen people,
and the British would have to go the way of all other
empires, in order to make way for the Jews. The Bible
said so !! And he slammed the cover of his closed Bible
with his hand in the most emphatic and impressive manner
possible. For a "loyal British subject" I could not help
thinking he was a little too enthusiastic about the prospec-
tive destruction of the British Empire! By the way, 1
have observed that it has become quite the fashionable
thing for preachers of sedition to preface their remarks
with declarations of their great loyalty; so ingenuous and
sincere are some of these simple-souled creatures, they
almost give you the impression that it is out of generosity
and magnanimity that they would turn the hearths and
homes of the British Islands over to the tender mercies
of Sinn Fein assassins. How generous we can be with the
lives and property of other people! Look out for the man
who opens his discourse with a declaration of his loyalty.
Methinks such a one protesteth too much. But, what queer
things the Bible can be made to say when it is kept shut!
Here was a closed Bible which was made to declare that
the only European power which had ever befriended the
Jew, was to be destroyed for the benefit of the Jew.
Logical, isn't it ? Destroy the British Empire to-morrow,
and what becomes of the Jew ? Will he ever possess
Jerusalem again ? Ask the Turk. Ask the Hun. Ask the
Red! Holding the views I do, I determined, if I ever found
time, to read up the subject as thoroughly as I was capable
of, and write about it, if for nothing else than to serve
notice on that type of cheap sensational preacher that a
closed Bible is no magician's wand. We expect Bibles to
be opened, read, and expounded. If the Bible says the
Empire is to be destroyed, then let us hear the worst and
get it over with. Where is the chapter and verse ? Per-

haps this is digression, but let it stand.

Secular and sacred history alike show that Ireland was peopled by the Phoenicians, and also by a people who settled in the North, and came to be known as the Tuatha da Danaan. I don't mind being dogmatic for once. This Tuatha da Danaan is part of the Tribe of Dan! I have given some of my scriptural proofs—more are to follow— and that is my conclusion. Not only mine, of course. It is the conclusion of eminent ethnological scholars, fully qualified to judge. Many of the proofs are inferential. True. But inferential proof, carefully weighed, is good proof. When the light streams in through your bedroom window, you infer that it is morning, and you conclude that the sun is shining without going out-doors to see it. Since the time of the Reformation, the light, feebly at first, but more and more strongly as developments ushered it in, has been breaking on the Anglo-Saxon race, and disclosing the proofs of their identity. Their identity existed before the Reformation, but the proofs, outside of the Scripture, did not exist. Some say Britain's greatness began with the Reformation. Quite true; but Britain, the "Covenant-Land," did not begin then. The Reformation was a necessary preliminary to Britain's greatness, but it was not the cause of it. It was then that the vine, long previously planted in the "goodly land" by "the great waters," began to spread and to bear its fruit. Why were not the British allowed to spread and expand into a great Empire while Britain was under religious allegiance to the Pope ? Do you ask why ? Well, the race which we claim to be, were commissioned to spread blessing to all nations of the earth; and while they were under the Roman Church they had no blessing to spread. That is the reason, as short as I can put it. That is the reason the spread and development of the Empire took place subsequent to the Reformation. Is it a sound reason or not ? God's dealings with

the world did not begin with the Reformation, large as
that event looms in our estimation. We must not put effect
before cause. This seems to be a good place in which to
answer the doubting objection put forward by many.
Namely: "If all this Identity Theory be true, why was it
not known long ago ?" This is easily answered. The identity Truth has been struggling to light within the last three-
quarters of a century or so. It would have been very
difficult to see it long ago, when there was no great wide-
spread Empire with its "nation and company of nations"
to fit into the picture portrayed in the sacred pages.

CHAPTER XVII.

It is fairly well known that the Irish people came from Spain; and I do not of course intend to dispute this fact. But, it may be asked, does not this make the Irish an originally Spanish race ? Oh, no! There is no such thing as a Spanish race. Spain was the birthplace of no race. Just here it will be as well also to write off the theory that the English—Angles and Saxons—are of German origin (Hunnish, as those grand pedigreed Sinn Fein-Fenian-Venetian-Phœnician-Philistine Irish fellow-countrymen of ours like to dub us). There is no German race either. Germany is not the birthplace of any race. The cradle of the races was in the East. The fathers of the races were Shem, Ham, and Japhet, the sons of Noah. The Saxons, who are a Semitic people, descended from Shem, as all good authorities prove; passed through Germany. True. Dwelt there for some time, a long time ? True. Came from Saxony in Germany to Britain ? True. Then the early Britons were Germans ? No, that's not true. Not a little bit of it. The early Britons, "Brith-ains" or "Covenant-men," were Saxons, "Isaac's-Sons," who while en route to their island home, dwelt in that part of Europe now included in Germany, so long that the region became known as Saxony or the land of the Saaks, Sakai, Sacæ, Sach-sens, or Saxons. I have touched on this before. I want to impress it now. The present people of Germany are believed to be the old Assyrians; but our story is not concerned with these.

To return to Spain and the Irish. How can we maintain that a people coming from Spain are Palestinians, that is, Hebrews and Phoenicians ? Well, why not ? The tribes of Dan and Simeon, as well as the Phoenicians, dwelt in the coast region of Palestine. They were engaged in mercantile marine traffic as the Bible unmistakably shows; the isles were settled by these merchants. Most certainly "the Isle" was replenished, that is, peopled, by the merchants of Phoenicia (Isa. 23.) Spain lies directly in the Mediterranean line of route between Palestine and the Isles of the North and West. Voyagers to parts unknown would naturally stop in Spain before venturing out into the Atlantic. We know that Saint Paul went to Spain, at a very much later date, of course. There is nothing in the fact that the Irish came from Spain, detrimental to the belief that they came first from Palestine. Indeed, it would be extremely unlikely, almost absurd, to think that they did not stop in Spain. Though some of them, quite possibly, sailed through the Straits of Gibraltar and made the voyage direct. Are there any traces of the "waymarks" of Dan in Spain ? Why, yes; there were the Dons, the old Spanish Grandees; superior again to the other people, as the Tuatha da Danaan were the superior race in Ireland. The Spanish Dons may have been Dans. I have no definite assertion to make about it; all I know is that Dan passed that way, and that he was strong on "waymarks". But I must not delay in Spain. We are in a hurry home, and there is a long story ahead yet. It will, I trust, be kindly borne in mind that this is not intended to be heavy history. You wouldn't read that; and so I am trying to make it an easy story. It was necessary to dwell a little on the Spanish-Irish theory, so that learners, beginning to see the light, may not be thrown into confusion should some wise-acre turn up and say, "That's all bosh. The Irish came from Spain, so they can't be Israelites!" Should anyone try to stop you with that, you might ask him if he thought people originally grew on the trees in Spain, and if it isn't Spanish chestnuts he is thinking about ? I heard from an old lady, who is now following this story very eagerly, that she was turned away

from the study about twenty years ago by an assurance
from her minister that the thing was "all bosh." Well,
to give it its honest due, the "bosh" argument is not very
persuasive. But it is fine to know that some of the best
exponents of this truth at the present time are bishops and
clergymen highly esteemed in churches of all denomina-
tions. They want unity in the churches! Perhaps it is in
this field that they shall find it! It should be remembered
that this is not a new religion. We have too many new
religions. It is not a religion at all, although it is closely
allied to religion inasmuch as it is a study of the Bible;
but anybody can take a hand, and you don't have to make
up a new Bible either, like the Russellites and the Mormons
and the Christian Scientists, and the What-nots. Oh, no!
You just study from the old Bible; that is the only condition
laid down. Also remember that we are all only students.
I want this understood, especially in regard to my own
writings; because, should I make any mistakes in my "inferential" proofs and conclusions, my mistakes do not af-
fect THE TRUTH in the least. There is the COVENANT!
That is the proof. As long as the covenant stands, and
that is "for ever," I am not worrying lest some of the
minor details of my little story are out. I may say I have
read lots of British-Israel writers with whom I do not
agree in some things; some of them no doubt will not agree
with me in everything; but we are not quarrelling, we are
all agreed on one thing—the everlasting covenant.

Let us take a brief glance at the "Dan-marks" of Ireland. Allowing for the change of vowels already explained, Ireland is full of Dan's marks. In addition to the Tuatha da Danaan, there are such names as Dundrum, Donegal,
Dundalk, Dangan, Dungarvan, Dungannon, etc.. etc., galore.
England and Scotland also have their Dan marks, all the
way from Dundee to London, including a river Don in
Scotland, and another in England. How long ago the

colonization and replenishing of the isles began is not
known, but historians place it as early at least as 900 years
before Christ. Just fix this in your mind. It means that
300 years before the Assyrian captivity, the British Islands
were settled and inhabited by Israelites of the tribes of Dan
and Simeon. It is very important to remember this. There
is, as we have seen, Scriptural proof of the fact that com-
mercial relations were fully established in the days of King
Solomon; and ships were passing regularly to and fro
about 300 years before the epoch of the Prophet Jeremiah.
The epoch of whom ? The Prophet Jeremiah, of course!

If Charles Dickens had only written this story he could
have handled it splendidly! He loved to gather lots of characters into his stories; and this is a tale that would have
supplied as many characters as he could have wished for.
Shortly we shall.have to introduce Jeremiah the Prophet;
yes, and Baruch the Scribe, and the Princess, and the Prince.
And Jeremiah will be the hero of this stage of the romance,
for, of course, the story contains a beautiful romance. This
does not mean, however, that we are going to indulge in
any "romancing" whatever. We shall stick to the truth,
as clearly as we can trace it, from Bible to legend, and
from legend to history; and if ever there was a story to
which the proverb applied that "Truth is stranger than
fiction" it is vindicated in this. But before we can enter
on this fascinating stage of our story, it will be necessary
for us to go back and pay due attention to another great
character whom we have not noticed very much so far. It
was not through oversight that we skipped over King David.
It seemed more convenient to dispose of the troublesome
tribe of Dan first, and to land them in Ireland, that is, the
coast or sailor part of the tribe, who, once again I will ask
you to remember, are now firmly established in this far off
island and are quite familiar with the ocean route back
and forth; so familiar with it that they would know just

where to steer for in a time of great danger in Palestine, should it ever be necessary for some of them to make a quick "get-away" on a very important mission or undertaking. That is all understood and settled. Now we shall have more leisure to go back and learn something about King David. The great King of Israel and Judah.

It will be necessary to go into those details of the life of King David with which every Sunday School scholar is thoroughly familiar. But, is there any passage in the life of David with which people are not familiar? We have from childhood known all about his early adventures, as the brave shepherd boy who slew a lion and a bear in defence of his father's sheep; his championship battle with Goliath when he slew the champion of the Philistines; the versatilities of his character and accomplishments as musician and sweet singer of Israel; his beautiful friendship with Jonathan; and finally, his call to the throne. Surely we know all about David! Yes, but if the average Bible reader were abruptly asked to state what he understood by the Davidic Covenant, what do you think the answer would be? The Davidic Covenant? Why, what do you mean by the Davidic Covenant? No, the Davidic Covenant is a subject which has not been dwelt upon over-much in the Sunday Schools. Well, the Davidic Covenant is to be found in 2 Sam. 7. It covers a whole chapter. The reader cannot do better than to read it over now. Read it more than once, for it is a tremendously important document. See what you can make out of it. The language could not be more clear, nor the covenant oath of God more binding. What does it mean? In the 10th verse there is the promise "Moreover, I will appoint a place for my people Israel, and will plant them that they may dwell in a place of their own and move no more." And, in the 16th verse, "Thine house and thy kingdom shall be established for ever before thee; thy throne shall be established for ever." This is the text of the Davidic Covenant, or God's Covenant with David. It is the complement of the Abrahamic Covenant.

Like the latter, it is all of grace, unconditional. Abraham, for God's purpose, was called out of Ur; and David was "taken from the sheepcote." It seems to harmonize with God's plan all through the Scriptures, "Ye have not chosen me, but I have chosen you." Now, what does this covenant exactly convey? Well, in the 10th verse it promises a permanent home and a "place of their own" to Israel; and, in the 16th verse, the House, Throne, and Kingdom of David is established for ever! Is it pedantry to insist on a distinction between these promises, as being made, part to Israel, and part to the King of the House of Judah personally? Certainly not. The word Israel is used in the first part of the covenant; and although at this time David was King of the twelve tribes, yet this part of the promise must have referred to the ten-tribed House of Israel only, because, otherwise, we would have to say that the great everlasting covenant, expressed with all the force Jehovah could put into words, had simply not been kept. We know that the poor Jews have no place of their own, and so far from moving no more, they have always been "on the move." But surely we cannot say the covenant is broken, when we remember that the Covenant-Maker is God. There are the people in "the Isles," so plainly indicated in other Scriptures as the part of Israel in whom this clause of the covenant is fulfilled.

But the second part of the covenant—the throne of David established for ever! Why, then, that must be the throne of the beloved Sovereign of "The United Kingdom of Great Britain and Ireland, and the British Dominions beyond the seas!" Yes, it means that, or our whole story falls to the ground.

CHAPTER XVIII.

In our last chapter we noticed that the Davidic Covenant has not been dwelt on over-much in the Sunday Schools. We, however, on the contrary, must go into it and discuss it somewhat fully, as it forms an extremely important part of our study. If we were to side-step this chapter we might as well admit that, although we had got along swimmingly up to this point, we sighted "breakers ahead" in the Davidic Covenant, and to avoid shipwreck we had to steer another course. We cannot do this, and so far from avoiding it as a dangerous rock, we propose to go straight ahead and pick it up, and take it along with us, for we could not get along without it.

Why has a chapter such as this been so sedulously avoided, while thousands and thousands of sermons have been devoted to impressing the comparatively ever so much simpler lessons to be learned from such stories as David's sling-stone victory over Goliath, and other like mere incidents of his career? I cast no disparagement on ever mere incidents when they are important enough to have been recorded in the Bible; but surely it is not common sense to devote all attention to incidents, and none at all to climaxes! I might enlarge on this, but to save space, you can think it it out for yourself.

The immense importance and the intense reality of the conveyances made in the Davidic Covenant may be realized better when we notice subsequent scriptures relating to it. It will be noticed that when God makes a promise, He always regards it as an event, and ever afterwards refers to it as something that has happened. Could this truth take

hold in the minds of Bible readers, generally, they would
not be so easily satisfied with any explanations as to why
God's promises are "not to be taken literally." "My
covenant will I not break, nor alter the thing that is gone
out of my lips." That does seem very emphatic, doesn't
it ? But surely, you say, no Christian people can be held
as teaching that God has broken His covenants ? Perhaps
not; but what about the charge that He has altered them ?
God makes the statement that He will neither break them
nor alter them.   I rather think the latter clause of the
statement has been somewhat overlooked.   None of us
would like it, if we had made a solemn promise to a particular friend, only to find that mutual friends had subsequently pulled our promise to pieces, and given it a totally
different meaning from that which the particular friend
to whom the promise had been made would naturally take!
Yet this is what has been done with God's promises to
David. They are held to have a spiritual meaning and not
a natural meaning. That is what the phrase "not to be
taken literally" amounts to.

One who has been accustomed to attaching only a
spiritual meaning to the Davidic Covenant would do well
at this point to read it over again, very carefully (2 Sam.
7) and then, lest he still thinks that he knows more about
it than David did, let him go on and read the both reminiscent and prophetic eighty-ninth Psalm, in which David sets
forth his recollections and impressions of its reality; his
very human fluctuations from exultation in the promise,
to despondency at the realization of sin and unworthiness;
from faith almost to despair, thence to prayer, hope and
trust.

"I have made a covenant with my chosen, I have sworn
unto David my servant. Thy seed will I establish for ever,
and build up thy throne to all generations,—in my name
shall his horn be exalted   I will set his hand also in the sea,

and his right hand in the rivers. I will make him my first-born, higher than the kings of the earth. My mercy will I keep for him for evermore, and my covenant shall stand fast with him. His seed also will I make to endure for ever, and his throne as the days of heaven. If his children forsake my law—I will visit their transgressions with the rod—Nevertheless my loving kindness will I not utterly take from him, nor suffer my faithfulness to fail. My covenant will I not break, nor alter the thing that is gone out of my lips—Once have I sworn by my holiness that I will not lie unto David. His seed shall endure for ever, and his throne as the sun before me. It shall be established for ever as the moon, and as a faithful witness in heaven." This in the words of the Psalmist himself is the astounding confirmation of God's covenant with him. It is as if he were inspired to bear witness as to what had taken place between him and his God.

After-generations, not apprehending its fulfilment, would be inclined to be skeptical about the covenant, to misconstrue it, to "spiritualize" it. Against these after thoughts and quasi-ripe interpretations, put forward "in the clearer light of the Gospel," and so forth, King David gives his own impression as the man on the spot at the time, and his interpretation of it, mind you, is to stand for all generations! It is quite against his testimony that its meaning has been altogether and absolutely changed in the course of the generations of Christendom. See what David says in the first verse of the Psalm—"With my mouth will I make known thy faithfulness to all generations." Now what authority have spiritualizers to change the testimony? What right had the writers of the heading of the chapter to introduce the word "Church" when such a word is not mentioned from beginning to end either of the Psalm or the Covenant which it confirms ? This covenant is not made about a church. It is made about a Throne, a regal House,

and a Kingdom. Before leaving this Psalm one might note
the climax and the anti-climax of the 37th and 38th verses.
The throne is exalted to the skies, up with the sun and the
moon, and then "abhorred," cast down to the ground.
Plainly "abhorred" because of the sin of idolatry, setting
in at the latter part of the erstwhile glorious reign of Solomon.   Thereafter the Psalm deals prophetically with the
castaway condition of God's people.   "How long, Lord ?
Wilt thou hide thyself forever ?"   How long ?   Oh it
would be a long, long, time; perhaps longer than David
dreamt of; and then there is gathering hope in the Singer's
mind when he invokes the memory of "thy former loving
kindnesses (the covenant) which thou swearest unto David
in thy truth;" and in the end there is trust and repose,
"Blessed be the Lord for evermore. Amen and Amen."
Surely it is a prophetic vision of the ups and downs of Israel.
Not a bad frame of mind for a man to arrive at, whose
thought and prayer is about an earthly kingdom, house and
throne ! Do you think it would be more edifying and spiritually beneficial had the Psalmist expressed himself to the
effect that after all it didn't matter very much even if
Rehoboam and Jeroboam made ducks and drakes of Israel,
and the kings of Assyria and Babylon took them captive,
as long as they all got to heaven in the end? I don't think it
would. Furthermore, I don't see why three-fourths of the
Bible is taken up with historical and prophetic references
to an earthly kingdom, throne, and people, if it be true that
such considerations are "too worldly."   In one of the
moods of even the most orthodox Christians among us, "to
make the world a better place to live in" is held to be a
most laudable aspiration; but in another mood, the mere
"world" is beneath their notice. Does it not occur to them
that the Maker of the world has His own plan for its destiny ? Is not the earth still the Lord's and the fulness
thereof ? the world; and they that dwell therein ? Has He

surrendered it to anybody ? How do you figure it out ? Here is a standing invitation to all readers to do their own thinking. You won't catch me using the phrase "Take it from me." No, if you are to get a lasting mental impression about anything you will have to think it out for yourself; then you can call it your own view, no matter who asked you to focus your attention on it.

An idea is held by some, that this Psalm was written by Ethan the Ezrahite, and not by David himself; but even were that the case it would be immaterial, for the words of the Psalm are ascribed to David; the impressions and aspirations are presented as his; it is pre-eminently a Psalm of David. My own belief, however, is that David is the author. The title, "Maschil of Ethan the Ezrahite", is explained by the marginal note—"Or, A Psalm for Ethan the Ezrahite to give instruction." Which seems to convey that it was written for Ethan, and not by him. Some of the Psalms were apparently written for leading singers; such as Ethan, Asaph, and Heman; to be used at special song services, when these leading singers and musicians would naturally "give instruction" to their respective groups or choirs. Such a special occasion, for instance, was the home-bringing of the Ark of the Covenant. (See 1 Chron. 15. What an organizer King David was!) This Psalm may very well have been written for a like occasion. I thought it well to add these remarks in regard to the authorship, as many are apt to be puzzled and confounded by quibbles as to who wrote such and such a chapter; how, where, and when. Well, after all, who knows ? Not the quibblers, certainly.

The idea you should avoid is that the Bible, as a study, is played out. People have asked me, what is the best book to study in order to "go deeper into the subject ?" There are many helpful books, but after all, the Bible itself is the main text-book and handbook of the whole matter; and, thank God! the Bible is common property. Read it for yourself. It is only the mentally lazy who are content to allow other people to do their Bible-reading for them; and then any fakir with a smooth voice or a ready pen can lead them around. We may, I think, assume that the translation of the Bible from the original Hebrew and Greek is about as perfect as human scholarship can make it. If you keep this fact in mind, you will not fall an easy prey to any upstart interpreter who comes along with a tale that "much of the Bible is spurious." Mrs. Baker Eddy wrote a "Key to the Scriptures," and the Christian Scientists had practically to drop the Scriptures. It takes them all their time to study the "Key." I read the "Key" through myself, so I know what I am writing about. I thought it was a Lock. Enter also the Mormons, with a second "inspired" Bible, a new prophet, new apostles, a new temple, and all up to date. Reader, I am not advertising these fungi, but I think it well to give them a side-long glance in passing; they are significant of the "latter days." "Through Thy precepts I get understanding, therefore I hate every false way. Thy Word is a lamp unto my feet and a light unto my path." Thy Word, God's Word itself, and not anybody's "key" to it. And that word must not be tampered with. (See Rev. 22: 18, 19.)

The study of God's dealings with His chosen people requires no new Bible, but on the other hand, it requires all there is of the old one. I think where this study differs from most others is, in that it begins with Genesis and goes clear through to Revelation. The best way to get a grasp of it is to take in the whole perspective. It will not be possible for us to see it all, but we can at least sense the fact that there is a profound plan underlying and permeating it all, and a purpose that has undergone no change. The God of Genesis is the God of Revelation. The same yesterday, to-day, and forever. The covenant which He made with

David is part and parcel of His plan of government for His world. When we realize that He established His covenant with David, fast as the Sun and the Moon for ever, we must see that as these heavenly bodies have not failed, then the House and Throne of David must have continued in Israel from that day to this, it will be for us to trace out how that covenant has been kept.

CHAPTER XIX.

Now, let us look back and take a brief glance at the
account of the birth of one of King David's ancestors. The
event is narrated in curious detail at the end of the 38th
chapter of Genesis. We read there about the birth of the
twin sons of Judah. Particulars are gone into; there is
the presentation of a hand, and the tying of a scarlet thread
around the baby's wrist by the midwife. Capable woman
apparently; she was fully alive to the importance in the
eyes of the Hebrew law of preserving the identity of the
firstborn. The turn of events did not find her unprepared;
there were twins, a moment's forgetfulness and it might be
impossible ever to know which baby was legally entitled
to the birthright, but she was ready with her scarlet thread
and the little hand was couped at the wrist. Yet this was
not the firstborn after all. The nurse, I imagine, was rather
indignant—present of mind, also ready of tongue, she ac-
costs the new firstborn infant with an accusation—"How
hast thou broken forth ? This breach be upon thee". And
"therefore" we read, "his name was called Pharez" (a
Breach). Then the other baby was born—the young knight
of the scarlet thread—"and his name was called Zarah" (a
Seed). And—Well, what then? Oh nothing. There isn't
anything more about it. The subject is dropped, after the
inscrutable manner of the Bible. Queer little old story to
have been preserved in Holy Writ down through the ages!
Wonder why it was narrated at all ? Curious names for the
babies, too—one a Breach, the other a Seed. Can any
significance be assigned to these names ? Hebrew names
usually had a meaning and a reason for their meaning.
Pharez was a direct ancestor in the line of David. Is it

possible that the midwife's exclamation was a prophecy?
Was there to be a breach in the kingly line of the far
distant future? That would account for Pharez, the
"Breach". Was the line to be saved from extinction by
some collateral descendant of him of the scarlet thread?
That would explain Zarah, the "Seed". But the Bible
drops the story without explanation. Let us do the same
for the present.

Now for a short summary of the specific conveyances
under the Davidic covenant. These are twofold (1) A
permanent place of their own, in which Israel is to dwell
in security; and (2) The establishment of the Kingdom and
throne of David for ever. This latter conveyance involves
the consequence that the House of Israel is to become the
Kingdom of David. It involves the resultant conclusion—
if the Bible be the Word of God—that, at the present time,
there must be in existence somewhere on this earth the
ancient nation of Israel, ruled over by a sovereign of the
Davidic line—that is, I mean, if the Bible be true—for we
cannot get outside the scope of the "forever"; and, by the
same token, this nation must be located in a place of quite
impregnable security. Not comparatively safe, but absolutely invulnerable. All kinds of dangers must have
been provided for in the prescience of a Mind which bes-
poke security "for ever" for His chosen people. Formid-
able armadas of galleons of war might essay the capture
of a secure place, such as we have in mind, only to be wrecked on its rocky shores. The conqueror of all Europe might
stand with folded arms and lowering brow gazing across
a certain channel, planning with that scintillating brain.
thinking the lightning thoughts of Napoleon. What might
he not do with a lot of rafts could he only get control of
that channel for twelve hours—Master of the channel and
he would be the master of the world! Just imagine it!
Such a prize to be so nearly within his reach. But the

greatest strategist in the world simply could not think
up a plan that would make the channel his own, even for
twelve hours.   Narrow channel, too, the one we have in
mind—men have swum across it.   But that "for.ever" is
a long time.   Many and strange are the dangers to be
countered by people holding such a lease.   The age of
invention would bring all manner of scientific appliances
into use.   A new enemy would occupy half a century amas-
sing an enormous assortment of machinery of destruction
in a volume unheard of.   There would be the Zeppelin, the
submarine, the poison gas, the monster guns throwing shells
70 miles, the strategic railways with mobile armies surging
at will from one theatre to another—armies in comparison
to which Napoleon's was a snail in pace and a corporal's
guard in size. Kaiser Wilhelm would succeed where Napoleon had failed!   Did he ?   Napoleon at least stood on the
shore and looked across; but the Kaiser, with all his jugger-
naut equipment, never got that near it.   No doubt he has
his reflections on what might have been, had he ever once
gained the channel ports.   It might have been, had it not
been pre-arranged by a Higher Command than the Kaiser's
that it was not to be.   The Zeppelin, the submarine, the
poison gas, the long-distance gun—all must fail.   Why ?
Because in the terms of the lease there is a clause that "No
weapon that is formed against thee shall prosper."   What
a comprehensive Mind it was that took apparent cognizance
of a coming age of invention!   Are we to be told that these
Bible passages are just "Hebrew records" ?   Would an
uninspired Hebrew writer in those primitive times use ex-
pressions which were hardly relevant to his own time, but
which ring almost uncannily true to the letter in these
"latter days" ?

     "No weapon that is formed against thee shall prosper"
(Isaiah 54:17). Read the whole chapter, for it is addressed
to the House of Israel in the time of their banishment.

Never mind what the heading says about a church. These headings are only the conceptions of old churchmen who felt that way about it; they are not part of the inspired word. No disparagement of the Church is intended, by the way. To prevent misunderstanding, I will say now that I am a member of the Anglican Church, with a strong preference for that form of Christian worship; chiefly, I think, because so much of the Bible is contained in the service, and so little is left to depend on the caprice of the Minister. Especially one must appreciate that wise twentieth article of religion, which lays down that "It is not lawful for the church to ordain anything that is contrary to God's word written, **neither may it so expound one place of Scripture, that it be repugnant to another.**"....In the view of the British national church, be it noted, the Bible is "God's word written." In the preface to the Book of Common Prayer it is arranged that the Old Testament, "the most part thereof", shall be read every year once; and "the New Testament shall be read orderly every year twice". A Methodist Minister criticises us, Anglo-Israelites, for "coming to the Bible with a naive faith." Why, yes, naturally so for my part. I am a Church of England man. The fact that we have so many Methodists with us, though, is evidence that my critic's views of the Bible are not in accordance with the tenets of the Methodist Church. However, we are not discussing forms of worship just now; the subject under consideration is the identity of the British people, and we are tracing it in the Bible; that is the reason we clash with the churchmen sometimes, because some of the churchmen are very insistent that "Israel" really means the Church; while we are propounding the probability that it means just "Israel". The mistake which the old fathers, Jerome and Origen, laboured under was not unnatural; they must not be too hastily condemned. It must be borne in mind that in their time there was no world-wide Anglo-Saxon race filling the place promised to Israel. There was nothing material in evidence, so, though they believed in the Bible, they gave every blessing a spiritual meaning and annexed them all on behalf of the Church. The promises will not fit the Church, of course, as we see now: a **nation** was stipulated, but at that time such a nation was nowhere in sight. The incongruity of it all is, that, while knowledge is advancing in all other spheres, the majority of Christendom are still willing to pin their faith to the views of the old fathers, who formed their judgment under the disability of lack of evidence. New evidence has come to light, an appeal against the old decrees is being asked for.

To those churchmen who believe the Bible to be "God's word written" there ought not to be anything repugnant in a belief which testifies to its literal as well as spiritual truth. Many have testified that this belief has intensified their interest in the Bible and shed a new light on whole sections of the sacred oracle, heretofore hardly intelligible. It is as contrary to common sense as it is to experience to think that this added clarity can dim the spiritual meaning. We do not for a moment set up the view that there is no spiritual meaning in the Old Testament promises; but you cannot spiritualize the terms of the Abrahamic and Davidic covenants to the exclusion of their literal meaning any more than you can spiritualize the Rock of Gibraltar. A great vista of destiny, however, is glimpsed when we entertain the thought that the literal is to merge into the spiritual, when time merges into eternity; that at the second coming of Christ for His millennial reign, the ancient people of Israel will be in existence, for they have been established "forever"; they shall at the moment of His coming be in the premier position as "chief of the nations". Then will the great voices proclaim that "The kingdoms of this world are become the kingdoms of our Lord and of His Christ:

and He shall reign for ever and ever". So says the Word of God in Revelation: it will be the climax of the covenants and the promises. I make no pretence in this little volume of explaining how the transfer of sovereignty from the earthly King of the House of David to our Lord is to come about. We know that our Lord Himself came of the line of David, and when the earthly king renders account of his stewardship and lays his crown at the feet of Jesus, the covenant shall suffer no lapse, the throne of David shall, without cavil, be "established forever." The theme might be the subject of volumes of conjecture, and one is conscious that it merges into the infinite. The Prophet Micah leads up to this climax with a wonderful harmony. (Micah 4.) "In the last days it shall come to pass." The millennial metropolis will be Jerusalem. "The law shall go forth from Zion, and the word of the Lord from Jerusalem." "Many nations shall come, and say, Come and let us go up to the mountain of the Lord, and to the house of the God of Jacob." "Many nations" shall be blest at the Divinely ap-pointed place of blessing. The old purpose of blessing for all nations still holds good. Yet is the sovereignty to remain with Israel—for, we read, "And thou, O tower of the flock, the stronghold of the daughter of Zion, unto thee shall it come, **even the first dominion; the kingdom shall come to the daughter of Jerusalem.**" The kingdom, the first domin-ion, the sovereignty—all are to remain for ever the portion of the "Tower of the Flock", the nation which has borne the brunt of the white man's burden.

CHAPTER XX.

In our last chapter we considered Great Britain's right to the title of a place of safety wherein God's people Israel might dwell secure; we saw how it has been proved to demonstration at least three times. Philip of Spain, Napoleon, and the Kaiser, each in his turn fell on that rock and was broken. The latest failure was the most colossal: the prophecy that no weapon formed against Israel shall prosper has been signally exemplified. On grounds of logic alone then the identity of the location is established. It will not be necessary for me to strain any great effort to prove how the people got there. Does it matter very much if we are not able to explain each step to those who would not believe in any case, no matter what? Is it reasonable to say to us—This thing cannot be, because you are not able to account for each move of a wandering people who left their native land seven hundred years before Christ? (Ages before the era of printing). Because you are not able to produce any log book left by the wanderers? Is it reasonable? It was to the idolatrous and banished House of Israel that the Lord said "Therefore, behold I will hedge up thy way with thorns, and make a wall, that she shall not find her path." My critic says there are gaps in the story! Well, then, we see that God Himself covered the trail of His people through the wilderness, so it was impossible to find it, until such time as He chose to make the revelation. The revelation has, in fact, been made by the exposition of a nation, a company of nations, and a people, in the precise position and answering every single description without exception that has been made of the people Israel. The whole panorama is laid out before anyone

whose eyes are open. The Bible indicates that there are
final revelations and demonstrations in store, such demon
strations as will not require any considerable time to usher
in their fulfilment, beholding which all shall be forced to
see that God's word is vindicated and His will accomplished: "Sing, O ye heavens; for the Lord hath done it; shout,
ye lower parts of the earth: break forth into singing, ye
mountains, O forest, and every tree therein, for the Lord
hath redeemed Jacob, and glorified Himself in Israel."
Isa. 44: 23.

'Tis like grovelling in the mire to seek to find Israel's
pathway through secular channels, when we have the magnificent language of Isaiah calling on us to recognize the
fait accompli. A passage from Dr. Latham's "Ethnology
of Europe" is often quoted by British Israel writers, as
follows:—"The eponymus of the Argive Danai was no other
than that of the Israelite tribe of Dan; only we are so used
to confine ourselves to the soil of Palestine in our consideration of the Israelites, that we treat them as if they were
adscripti glebae, and ignore the share they may have taken
in the ordinary history of the world.' The seaports of Tyre
and Ascalon, of Dan, Ephraim, and Ashur, must have followed the history of seaports in general; and not stood on
the coast for nothing. What a light would be thrown on
the origin of the name Peloponnesus, and the history of
the Pelop-id family, if a **bona-fide** nation of Pelopes, with
unequivocal affinities and contemporary annals had existed
on the coast of Asia! Who would have hesitated to connect
the two? Yet with the Danai and the Tribe of Dan this is
the case and no one connects them." Dr. Latham, the
erudite ethnologist had, it seems, got as far as connecting
the Dannai of Greece with the tribe of Dan. My critic
talks about "well known conclusions of ethnological history"; he accuses us of "setting them aside"; yet, despite
Dr. Latham to the contrary, he tells us that the ten Northern

tribes of Israel "were lost by complete assimilation".
(My critic's letter will be found at the end of the book,
we shall take it to pieces as we go along). I do not know
if Dr. Latham ever thought of such a namesake of the
Dannai and the Tribe of Dan, as the Tuatha da Danaan of
Ulster, a people of Eastern origin, coming from the same
region as the Dannai and the tribe of Dan—surely his logic
would apply to identify the relationship. On consulting a
Gaelic Bible I find that the word "Tuath" means "North";
so that there is not much hazard in asserting that the name
Tuatha da Danaan might be literally translated into the
"Dans of the North"; if not, will my critic give a better
explanation of the origin of the name ? Will he suggest
that they were Teutons, and then refer to the suggestion
as "This nemesis of fact"? All Scriptural prophecies point
to the British Isles of the North and West; and I am glad
to quote Dr. Latham in proof that "the conclusions of
scholars" are not opposed to the literal acceptance of the
Bible as the Word of God; it appears that it is not we who
are setting the scholars at naught. Nor must we allow any
modern autocrat of the pulpit lightly to "set aside the well
known conclusion" of all Christendom, gentle and simple,
scholar and ignorant alike ; that the Bible is inspired. If we
can't believe the Bible, then what's the use of anything ?
We may as well go fishing Sundays. I am not giving my
critic's name—he may want to use it again—I have a personal opinion of my own, though, about a supposed Minister
of the Gospel who becomes so obsessed with the superiority
of his own logic as to ask people to accept it in preference
to the Bible. When a man finds himself getting top
heavy like that, he should do something else for a living;
in the interests of religion I do aver that his place in the
pulpit would be better filled by a vacuum.

There has been, as we have seen, no modern invasion
of the British Islands. The old invasions were but the

home-comings of the different tribes; the long last and illustrious Tribe of Benjamin being accounted for in the Norman invasion of 1066. We know that Benjamin had been left behind "as a lamp unto Jerusalem"; and this great tribe had, necessarily, to be added to their brethren. We know from history that each succeeding levy of invaders was in a comparatively short space of time absorbed into the body politic, not as conquerors but as compeers, and nobody had to move out, that is, none of the British. The Romans, of course, had to go. Why was this? Well, you see, that is the way the decree was worded. They were to come to a place of their own, and move no more. While before that, they had been the greatest rovers ever. Scythians, or wanderers, they were in name and in fact. Then, for a time, the national character seems to have undergone a change. But note you, it is all according to the book. I want your sympathetic intelligence here. If you are a believer, is it not beautiful? If you are not yet a believer, is it not still remarkable? These Scythians were going by the book when they wandered, restless, to and fro in the wilderness to which they had been "allured," drifting slowly nearer and nearer, drawn home by some magnetism, or driven home by circumstance as some were, they all finally arrived. It was not a peaceful home-coming by any means; there was a fierce fighting between the different tribes: and indeed the different tribal characteristics still exist between the people now known as Welsh, Scotch, English, and Irish: nevertheless there was an ultimate settling down, and a great temporary change came over the nation. Going by the book again, as it is written, "Keep silence before me, O Islands; and let the people renew their strength". The great purpose of their national existence as the chosen people of God lies ahead. They have need to renew their strength for there is a world of work before them.

"Surely the isles shall wait for me"! Yes, we might weave many thoughts around that. Let us have a practical thought. Benjamin had been detained in Palestine, for David's sake, to be a light in Jerusalem. Benjamin would have to wait, at any rate, 720 years after the others had departed. He must wait for the dawn of Christianity. He would then be equipped with the light shining in a dark place. It is strongly believed that it was this tribe which furnished all the apostles, not counting Iscariot: the eleven were Galileans; St. Paul also was a Benjamite. These were they who ultimately received the commission to go forth and make disciples of all nations, being sent first to the **"Lost sheep of the House of Israel"**; but I want to connect you with the thought I have in mind. Benjamin must wait in Jerusalem to be equipped to do God's work. So God would say to the people in the Isles in turn, "Surely the Isles shall wait for me". "I am holding one of your brethren on a mission of my service. You must wait until I have equipped him as a 'light bearer' to the regions beyond". One must not presume to say what thought the Almighty had in mind, or ascribe reasons. But from a human stand-point this would be a practical reason for commanding the Isles to wait, before spreading abroad. as they were to do later. They must wait for Christianity: and, while waiting, they would "renew their strength", that is, establish by centuries of gradual growth and development the rugged character that is British. Thwarted, buffetted and battered on the anvil of a nation's long experience they were; until we have the most stable, the most stolid, the most patient with experience, and withal the most honourable national character in the world, in John Bull. His character is not of mushroom growth; he did not arrive at manhood overnight. Nor did Benjamin reach home in a year!

I cannot attempt in this volume to go into details of

Benjamin's adventures in the thousand years of his pilgrimage. They received a prophetic warning by Jeremiah (Chap. 6:1) "O ye children of Benjamin, gather yourselves to flee out of the midst of Jerusalem—for evil appeareth out of the North, and great destruction." Study of the context will show that this is a prophecy as well as a warning. It was a laying down of the course to be taken by Benjamin when the predicted crisis had arrived, that is, when the evil should "appear out of the North"—obviously the flight of Benjamin was not to take place until the set time, for Benjamin must yet tarry in Jerusalem until equipped with the light of which he was to be the bearer. Jeremiah's prophetic warning was uttered some 620 years before Christ; the flight of Benjamin was not to take place until after the lapse of the intervening centuries. The "evil" and "great destruction" appearing out of the north would appear from the sequence of events to have been the Northern power of Rome. Benjamin fled from Jerusalem before the city was destroyed by Titus in A.D. 70, and started on their long journey to the new promised land. From 70 to 1066 A.D.—A thousand years is to Him but as a day! "Surely the Isles shall wait for me"—And Benjamin!

"I go to prove my soul. I see my way as birds their trackless way.

I shall arrive! What time, what circuit first, I ask not. But unless God send his hail or blinding fireballs, sleet or stifling snow, in some time, His good time, I shall arrive. He guides me and the bird. In His good time."

In 1066 Benjamin arrived as William the Conqueror, with a wolf displayed on his banner—as it is written, "Benjamin shall ravin as a wolf." He had been long detayed but he arrived with the characteristic rush, there was the quick clash and the desperate struggle at Hastings and it was over. The phenomenon is repeated: the Norman is absorbed by the English and the Briton. Nobody moves out, but all have arrived home. We notice how comparatively easy it was for these home-comers to invade the country; but from that day to this the feat has proven impossible—Why ? Well, I should say because ''So it is written.''

But some may ask : Is it possible to prove from **History** that the Normans are actually the Tribe of Benjamin ? A school master in Gloucestershire, England, wished me to state if I knew of any history book definitely connecting the Saxons with the Israelites. He did not know of any such history, but added, ''that was not to say that none such was in existence.'' Another friend, an insurance man, said he would like to believe the British-Israel theory, and he would believe it if I could show him a plain statement, in the Bible or in history, that the ten tribes went from Palestine to the British Islands. He actually would believe it then. That man won't take many bad risks! Now to my school master friend I would say, that he has no need to add such a modest qualification to his query. If any such history book were in existence he would certainly be likely to know more about it than I would. But surely such querists will admit that if either the Bible or recognized history gave an explicit account of the travels of the exiles, and named their destination, then the term ''lost tribes'' would be a misnomer. Christ's own reference to the lost sheep of the House of Israel would have had no meaning. As we have already fully noted, the Bible shows that they were banished by reason of, and in punishment for, their sins; and being scattered hither and thither, they gradually lost consciousness of their identity, and so became ''the lost tribes''. But the Bible also shows that their wanderings were to be guided and over-ruled by that purpose which had appointed their destiny. They were to be gathered in an Island home, where they were to wait for Christianity. Nor does history show anything to the contrary. Nay, rather, it furnishes what we regard as strong inferential proofs. History, then, should give us one tribe invading Britain many centuries later than the others. History gives us the Normans.

Paul de Chaillu, in "The Viking Age", traces the Normans back to the region of the Crimea and the shores of the Black Sea. The location of the captivity of the ten tribes was in the land of Media. Sharon Turner, the historian of the Anglo-Saxons, quotes Strabo, Herodotus, and other accepted authorities in proof that the Anglo-Saxons came from Media. Josephus and Esdras also tell us that the ten tribes disappeared into the same region from which the Anglo-Saxons emerge. We know that other races also came into Europe over the same route; our opponents have a supercilious way of reminding us of this, as if we were not aware of it. We are. We have no intention of monopolizing the thoroughfare; but, let me say shortly: **The others haven't arrived.** The conclusion of our opponents, however, is that the ten tribes never started; that they alone of all nations remained behind, slumped, melted away, what you will! And, incidentally, that Josephus didn't know what he was talking about.

Other writers, like Major Weldon, in his "Origin of the English", have catered amply for those who require historical detail: such detail is, of course, most interesting. But for my part, in this little sketch, it will be remembered that I am basing my argument on what I call the major premiss—that is, the Covenant—and, to this line of argument, the historical corroborations, though intensely interesting, are not vital. Also the "conclusions of scholars" that run counter to the Covenant are mistakes, and not very innocent mistakes at that. They are examples of cases where "A **lot** of learning is a dangerous thing." I use that paraphrase advisedly. I mean it is a dangerous thing

for the masses of the people when the authority of the
Bible is impugned in the pulpit. Nor is it a logical thing
for these "scholars" to do. They might reflect that
it is metaphysically impossible for them to bestow
their ultra-scholarship on the masses, to compensate
them for that faith in God which they are under-
mining and filching away. Greek will always be Greek to
the masses. The higher critics would have people look
askance at the Bible, though they have nothing to offer
in its place. That is exactly what the higher critics are
doing. Bill Jones did not read his Bible over-much, yet
at least he knew what it was; that is, he thought he did,
but with so many theological fog horns blowing, Bill is in
danger of losing his bearings. That's what the "higher
critics" are doing to Bill Jones. Howbeit Greek has met
Greek in the halls of learning, and it were a mistake to
suppose that the prerogative of scholarship pertains ex-
clusively to the "higher critics". They have, in fact, only
a part of it.

We have seen that it would be absurd to expect a statement in the Bible specifically naming the country in which
the "lost tribes" were to be found; yet we have many explicit statements directly contradicting the theory that they
were to pass out of existence: "I will sift the House of Israel
among all nations, like as corn is sifted in a sieve, yet
shall not the least grain fall upon the earth." That is Amos
9:9. Yet my clerical critic has the effrontery to cite Amos,
while he makes the statement, on his own authority, that the
tribes "were lost by complete assimilation"; giving the lie
direct to the Scripture which says, "He that scattered
Israel will gather him and keep him, as a shepherd does his
flock". He also gives the lie to James, who addresses his
epistle to the "Twelve Tribes scattered abroad." Perhaps
James had not studied the circumstances from which the
"well known conclusions of the scholars" are drawn, and

so was not aware that ten of the tribes had been assimilated out of existence. Christ also—under a misapprehension, when He sent His disciples on the vain quest of Lost Sheep, who could not possibly be found because they had ceased to be. This higher criticism is great stuff.

CHAPTER XXI.

"Keep silence before me, O islands, and let the people renew their strength: let them come near; let them speak; let us come near together to judgment" (Isaiah 41). Who are the people ? "Thou Israel art my servant, Jacob whom I have chosen, the seed of Abraham my friend. Thou whom I have taken from the ends of the earth." (Verses 8, 9). This indicates who the people are, where they are, why they were chosen, and what they were chosen for. They are the seed of Abraham—now dwelling on islands. gathered in from "the ends of the earth"—chosen because their ancestor Abraham was God's friend—and chosen for service. "Thou, Israel, art my servant." Fore-appointed to fulfill the service entailed on the seed of Abraham—"In thy seed shall all the nations of the earth be blessed, because thou hast obeyed my voice." Gen. 22:18.

Surely it is contempt; it is "lese majeste", to ascribe to these enunciations the vagueness of allegory. It is God bearing witness that He is mindful of His covenant and true to His original purpose.

But how was it to come about that these Baal-worshippers should be a blessing to other nations ? Look at that first verse again. "Let us come near together to judgment." Ah yes! when they judged themselves from or near God's view-point there would be sad reflections and heart-searchings; and at the end would be a decision. Hosea tells us how they would voice it: "I will go and return to my first husband, for then was it better with me than now." But is not this treating the Almighty with off-hand assurance ? Can the "First Husband" in justice take these divorced adulterers back ? Yes, for He has devised a plan whereby "Righteousness and peace have kissed each other"

—"Fear not, thou worm Jacob, and ye men of Israel, I will help thee, saith the Lord, and THY REDEEMER THE HOLY ONE OF ISRAEL". Verily might our blessed Lord say, "Search the Scriptures—they are they which testify of me". (Our Lord of course referred to the Old Testament scriptures). How far have you carried the search, my friend? Have you been allowing the "higher critic" to do the searching for you? Have you discovered that there is no barrier between God and each one of us individually, and our nation, nationally, but our own stubborn will? Well indeed might the high priest prophesy that "Jesus should die for that nation (the Jews) and not for that nation only, but that also he should gather together in one the children of God **that were scattered abroad**". The inference here is that these "children of God" had been worshippers of Him in Palestine, with "that nation", but were now scattered abroad. "He that scattered Israel will gather him—for the Lord hath redeemed Jacob". Behold the Way of the gathering! Christ says "I am the way"—"Search the scriptures". "Let the children first be fed": "I am not sent but unto the lost sheep of the House of Israel". These first. First in blessing, and first in responsibility. They in turn should carry the blessing to "all nations"; "Thou art my servant, O Israel, in whom I will be glorified". But the Devil has perverted Christendom with a counterfeit humility, to the effect that it is all arrogance and bombast, and that there is nothing special in the way of service expected from the Anglo-Saxons. It would be arrogance did we claim that we were fulfilling our part of the contract of our own volition as well as we ought. We are indeed in a great measure fulfilling it from force of circumstances; but as for the plan, it was not ours. It was the Almighty who originated the scheme of chosing "two families" for His service. (Jer. 33:24). **It was His plan.** The only question for us is—Are we going to stand

up to the plan ? Noblesse Oblige ! Humility is a virtue;
but we know what God thinks of the brand of humility
which finds a man unearthing a napkin at the last and
returning a rusty talent to the Giver. I repeat, it is God's
plan that the "higher critics" are sneering at.

It will be useful to draw a few comparisons between
what happened in Britain, subsequent to the gathering in
of the Scythian wanderers, and what was predicted to
happen to Israel. First, as we have seen, there was the
Redemption and conversion to Christianity. Here is the
line of demarcation between Israel and Judah. "The people found grace in the wilderness, even Israel, when I went
to cause him to rest". Through Isaiah God tells us that
the people, Israel, were in the islands, "to renew their
strength", and through Jeremiah, that they were "caused
to rest in the wilderness". In Isaiah again the people in
the islands were to "come near to judgment" by grace of
their Redeemer; while in Jeremiah "the people, even Israel,
found grace in the wilderness". The people, then, are the
same, "even Israel". The fact proclaimed is the same:
Israel "found grace" in the wilderness and in the isles.
They had been "allured" into the wilderness and "caused
to rest" when they came to the islands at the uttermost
end of the wilderness. They say these are just Hebrew
records; so be it for the moment; then they record the fact
that there are Israelites on earth other than the Jews—
**for the latter were never allured into the wilderness, nor
have they yet "found grace".** Thus far, the description
of the British Islanders and Israel is identical. It is no
far-fetched theory to assume that "finding grace" here
meant conversion to Christianity. It is the grace of the
Redeemer that is plainly specified. Our critics accuse us
of drawing on our imagination. Well, thanks be to God,
if we have an imagination to draw upon! "Where there
is no vision the people perish." Yes, let us exert all our

powers of intellect as we read the Bible. Let us "imagine" that it reaches up higher and down deeper than the croak of the so-called "higher critic", and wider than the tabulated formulæ, which seek to supplant consideration of God's personal dealings with His creation, by a cold analysis of the influence of spirit over matter. Israel could never carry out his mandate to bless the heathen with that sort of stuff. The heathen wouldn't understand it in the first place, and even if they did they wouldn't be blest. Ever hear of a higher critic in the foreign mission field ? No, they hang around the clubs at home.

The people settled down in the islands "to renew their strength". Settled down for ever ? By no means. That was not the destiny appointed for Israel. They were to spread abroad far and wide. Impelled by the conviction that they were God's chosen people ? Oh no ! They were probably impelled by all kinds of motives. The one most popularly ascribed is the spirit of adventure, and perhaps that was the primary motive, for we have been an adventurous race. As sailors ! The floors of the seven seas are strewn with dead Britons.

> "The spirits of your fathers shall start from every
>   wave
> For the deck it was their field of fame, and the
>   ocean was their grave".

As soldiers ! We have crossed swords with everybody. It is British soldiers who have been everywhere and done everything; as the song has it, "Who've been, my lads ! Who've seen, my lads !" Their achievements have been such that a mere recital of them without giving an impression of boasting would be difficult. Not a desert strand in the world but holds in its bosom the bones of British soldiers. But I waste time; you know all this. Yes ? Then you know that, for some reason or other, the British have done exactly the things foretold for the Israelites. I was just leading you up to another text—"Enlarge the place of thy tent, and let them stretch forth the curtains of thine habitations: spare not, lengthen thy cords, and strengthen thy stakes: For thou shalt break forth on the right hand and on the left; and thy seed shall inherit the Gentiles, and make the desolate cities to be inhabited." (Isaiah 54:3).

"Thou wilt perform the truth to Jacob and the mercy to Abraham, which thou hast sworn unto our fathers from the days of old." So wrote the prophet Micah, a thousand years after Jacob had told his sons what TRUTH it was that God had sworn unto him; yet Micah speaks of it as still in the future. The TRUTH had evidently not been performed in Micah's day. Then, when is God to perform this truth? Let us naturally ask Jacob to name the time. Jacob says "In the last days"! "Gather yourselves together ye sons of Jacob that I may tell you that which shall befall you in the last days." Well, the last days are here; we look for the sons of Jacob expecting to find them in the great position predicted, and lo! we see John Bull, standing on the right hand and on the left; strong in the east and in the west; his triple crossed flag floating in all climes, from the arctic circle to the antipodes; from the centre of civilization "unto the utmost bound of the everlasting hills"; having "the heathen for an inheritance", by the hundreds of millions: ruling in righteousness, carrying the blessing of freedom and the gospel to "all nations"; possessing the "blessings of the deep"—the great sea-going nation: answering all the descriptions—"From the top of the rocks I see him, and from the hills I behold him: lo, the people shall dwell alone, and shall not be reckoned among the nations. Who can count the dust of Jacob, and the number of the fourth part of Israel?" (Num. 23: 9-10).

What say you, my friend, do we look for another?

The passage I have purposely chosen contains a sentence which is often cited as a supposed refutation of our belief— "The people shall dwell alone, and shall not be reckoned among the nations"—the contention being that such language could not apply to the British, as it implies a people living by themselves, and **not a nation**; but it would apply to the Jews. Possibly, if you took that clause out of the context and forgot all the other descriptions, you might reason that way. But surely that would be a stupid thing to do. What has the context done to you! Why forget the other prophecies that these same people were not only to be a nation but "the chief of the nations", which by this contention is admitted could not be the Jews! Supposing our critics were honestly seeking the truth, instead of looking for catch words to get the better of an argument, they would read whole chapters and take texts in consideration with the context, and be gracious enough to allow the books of the Bible the coherency which they readily concede to other books. One might take a phrase out of a man's letter, and construe from it a meaning altogether apart from the arguments which led up to it, or the conclusions which followed. In a court of justice such fragmentary reading of documents would not be admitted as evidence. Well, then, if you want to do justice to God's Book you will be governed by the same rule—give it British fair play. Taking the whole of this text with the setting of the chapter, the obvious meaning is that so great would be the people that they would "stand alone", an **outstanding nation**; not "reckoned among the nations", but head and shoulders above them, as becomes "the chief of the nations". Is this distortion? No, but any other view would be; the whole chapter depicts greatness; if this text were held as implying that God's people were not to be a nation, it would simply give the lie to the everlasting covenant of great nationhood. Some people make no bones

about giving the lie to the covenant; but I am only bringing out the fact that they cannot quote scripture against it.

Ah yes ! "From the tops of the rocks I see him"—
everywhere, a nation "dwelling alone", outstanding, "not
reckoned with the nations"—Isra-El. "Who can count
the dust of Jacob, and the fourth part of Israel ?" I am
tempted to compare the metaphor of this text with a saying of some British statesman—I forget which—"There
are actresses, good, bad and indifferent and Sarah Bernhardt." Had he added that Bernhardt "stood alone" his
meaning would still be quite plain, and nobody would say
he meant that she was no actress! So one might appro-
priately say "There are nations, small, great, near great,
and the British"; and everybody would know what you
meant if you added "Britain stands alone". Perhaps some
will say this is "bombast"; let be; it is the truth, is it not ?
As to the bombast and the arrogance; wait a minute; we
may see if that cap does not fit our opponents.

CHAPTER XXII.

In the first chapter of Jeremiah it is stated that, before he was born, he was sanctified and ordained for a special service. He was to be a prophet to the nations (verse 5) and his direct commission is delivered in the 10th verse. "See, I have this day set thee over the nations, and over the kingdoms, to root out, and to pull down, and to destroy, and to throw down, TO BUILD, AND TO PLANT."

I have put the latter clause in big type (1st) because it is the part which is derided by our opponents, and (2nd) because it is the crux of my whole story. We all know about the rooting out and destroying of the kingdom of Judah. That is admitted to have been literal. Preachers have been wont to moralize on it. For disobedience and sin, say they, the kingdom of Judah was rooted out and destroyed; and the lesson for us to-day is to be obedient, and so avoid a like fate. So, So! And God thought so little of His oath to David that He broke it. So little of His chosen people, or rather so little of the great purpose of their choice, that He abandoned that plan, thereby tacitly acknowledging an error of judgment on His part in having ever devised such a plan. So little of all this has The God of Israel thought, and so much of us, that he overthrew everything just to provide us with an object lesson! When you sift that notion to the bottom after all you find that it is a great big smug notion about ourselves and our own importance. We are too humble to think that we may be His chosen people; but not too humble to think that God overthrew His chosen people, and abandoned His one plan for this world's government, just to suit our modern ideas. This is where the arrogance and the "pomposity" lies. I knew we should find it. The cap belongs to the Uriah Heeps of theology. Let them wear it.

Question—Suppose that worship is of any value to the Almighty; could He afford to advertise Himself to humanity as One who has had to shape His designs by experiment and alter His plans from time to time to suit the exigencies of occasion, after the manner of any other victim of circumstance ? We are, after all, creatures of intelligence. The idea of a victimized Deity does not align with our concept of Omnipotence; therefore we refuse to worship the god of the so-called "higher critics". Higher Criticism— I don't know where it gets its altitude — may succeed in destroying the faith of many, but, rest assured, its high priests are not destined to head any long procession into a new faith. Their way leads to atheism. We will worship a God that is a Revelation, but, at this late day, excuse us if we balk at a god that is a product of the colleges. They say the Bible is not the Word of God, as we supposed; very well: we refuse to build new altars.

Hark at the arraignment of the Bible by the higher critics—"Failure of prophecy", say they, "particularly of prophecy relating to the Hebrews, proves that the Bible is not the Word of God, but merely records of the Hebrews, inspired by a glorified and sentimental patriotism"—That is a fair synopsis of a contention that is damned by the word of Christ Himself, who says—"Think not that I am come to destroy the law, or the prophets . . . Till heaven and earth pass, one jot or one tittle shall in no wise pass from the law, till all be fulfilled." It is therefore not apparent why the higher critics are masquerading in vestments as Ministers of the Gospel, nor is it clear whose gospel it is that they preach. The expression, "Till heaven and earth pass", harmonizes well with the symbol used by God as a token of His pledge to David. "My covenant shall stand fast with him . . . his throne as the days of heaven. Once have I sworn by my holiness; I will not lie unto David; his seed shall endure for ever . . . and his throne as the sun before me." We conclude that our Saviour's testimony is a blanket confirmation of all scriptural promises, and surely it does not exclude the covenant, thus so emphatically sworn to. Has it all been superseded? Why no, not yet! I am writing this on Empire Day, 1921, and the sun, God's witness, is shining very brightly: I am grateful to believe that his beams are resting everywhere upon the banners of Israel. There is good scriptural foundation for the old saying that the sun never sets on the British Empire!

Now the "higher critics" are opposed by many sincere Christians, in and out of the gospel ministry, who strive to defend the Bible and "the failure of prophecy" with the old plea that it is not to be taken literally, but spiritually; and all is clear when we make some necessary changes in the text; as, for instance, interpolating the word "Church" in place of Israel, whenever any blessings are predicted; but being careful to allow the original word "Israel" to take the brunt of any judgments that are pronounced against that nation. A one sided contract truly! On whose authority? I don't know. Do you? Yet they will tell you quite blandly, and apparently with as much sincerity as if they had no mental reservations in regard to parts of it, that they believe the Bible is true. Surely that is a poor defence. I do not by any means put the spiritualizers in the same category as the "higher critics'"or faith destroyers. But I do commend to their earnest consideration a thesis which sets forth the fact that the prochecies relating to Israel have been, and are being, literally fulfilled to Britain; which involves the corrollary, not that the prophecies to Israel have failed, or been diverted to another, which is the same thing; but that, **ipso facto**, Britain is Israel. Here at once is a real defence of the Bible, a tribute to the faithfulness of God, and a confirmation of faith. Why are the spiritualizers afraid? And, again, just where do they draw the line between the literal and the spiritual? The banishment of Israel was literal; why not the restoration? This brings us back to our text.

We believe that Jeremiah got his commission to "pull down and root out", then we must, on the same authority, believe that he was commissioned to "build and to plant". It is in the same chapter and the same verse. Now what would he build and plant unless it be the seed of that which was rooted out? This must follow for the reason that had Jeremiah's mission ended at the rooting out and pulling down of the throne of Zedekiah, who sat on the throne of David, then God's covenant with David would have been broken. But where did he plant the seed, and build anew the throne of David? In another land, obviously, as it was to be rooted out of Palestine, and when we remember that the promise is not that the kingdom of the House of Judah should be again set up, but that "David shall never want a man to sit upon the throne of the **House of Israel**"; we look at once to the Isles of the North and West—the British Isles, to be exact, branded with their Hebrew name, the Isles of the Covenant-People—God appeals to Israel in the Isles; thither of necessity must we look for the new location of the throne of David, which is to endure as long as the sun shines.

Jeremiah the prophet, as the Bible student will know, was a son of Hilkiah, a priest of the tribe of Benjamin, allied at this time with the House of Judah: while the main body of the House of Israel had disappeared into captivity and beyond into the "wilderness". Some of them had never been in captivity though. Part at least of the tribe of Dan were in Ireland; we have already established this as a reasonable fact; and I believe the descendants of Zarah, the twin son of Judah, were then in Ireland. Some trace the "Red Branch Knights" of Ulster to this origin. In this connection I quote the following from Professor Odlum's book, "God's Covenant Man"—

"One hundred years or more ago Joseph Ben Jacob, a Celt and a Catholic, in a work called "Precursory Proofs", said:—Among the five equestrian orders of ancient Ireland was one called 'Craobh-Ruadh', the Red Branch. The origin of this Order was so very ancient that all attempts at explanation have hitherto failed. Some suppose that it originated from the Ulster Arms, which are Luna, a hand sinister **couped at the wrist**—Mars."

Which throws us back on another question—How did the Ulster Arms originate? All we know positively is that these things loomed up out of the mists of legend, and were in established existence before history writing became the custom. Of course I am one of those **who believe** that the Ulster Arms originate, as far as the hand is concerned, with the scarlet thread which the nurse tied around the baby's wrist. These things must have had a beginning, since they certainly had existence: we are really sorry that we cannot give day and date; but perhaps our critics have the solution? Is there something "wise" behind the smile of superiority with which they regard the Anglo-Israelites?

It is known, however, that long prior to the days of Jeremiah there existed in Ireland a royal house with a line of kings dating back nobody knows how long, but from the historical fact that this royal house was centered in the Tuatha da Danaan, or Dans of the North, we may be justified in concluding that this particular line of kings originated with the advent of those early explorers and adventurous traders of the Tribe of Dan, and existed in Ireland contemporaneously at least with the reign of Solomon in Palestine. Be this as it may, Irish history establishes the fact that this kingly house reigned in Ulster in the days of Jeremiah, and that about the year 583 B.C. the reigning king was Eochaid the Heremon. Of whom more anon.

Jeremiah, as we have seen, was ordained a prophet unto the nations. A **prophet**? This indicates that he was to have relations with other than his contemporaries. I do not hold with my critic that prophecies have only to do with "the live issues of the day"—such a definition, the very antithesis of the word prophecy, is too unintelligent to waste time disputing.   And a prophet to the **nations?** What nations? All nations, I should say, and all peoples, in all times, from the days of the prophet down to the present. The word of the Lord which came to the prophets is the decree of "the Judge of all the earth", and it concerns the past, present, and future of all people. I am not indulging in generalities; if you want the text here it is:—"To wit, Jerusalem and the cities of Judah.................the king of Egypt and all the mingled people .... the kings of Tyrus and Zidon (by the Mediterranean sea) **and the king of the Isles which are beyond the sea.** ("The Sea" is always the Mediterranean). And all the kings of the North, far and near .... and all the kingdoms of the world which are upon the face of the earth" (Jer. 25: 15-26.) I don't think there can be anybody left out of this list, from which I conclude that all are to be affected by the commission of Jeremiah; not only the Hebrews, but "all the nations of the earth"; primarily the Hebrews I suppose, and necessarily all others. To apply this to the present day; does it clash with our belief? Measure it up and see. Assuming that some fundamental condition of prosperity or adversity pertains first to the British Empire, all nations in the world must feel its effects. A British Empire condition is a world condition and is destined to become increasingly so, for our numbers and our requirements are increasing. "When the Most High divided to the nations their inheritance ....He set the bounds of the people according to the number of the children of Israel."

But Jeremiah was to begin at Jerusalem and deliver an impeachment against "all the cities of Judah", the "house of Jacob", and "all the families of Israel". The opening chapters contain a recital of God's gracious dealings with His people, and a black record of their ingratitude; intermingled with impassioned pleadings, warnings of punishment, proffers of mercy, and prophetic promises. The people are left without excuse; yet one gathers that the Lord, "declaring the end from the beginning", knew that generation would not repent, and the forecast of blessing relates to a distant future and to a redeemed people—"In those days" and "at that time"—not the days then present. "In those days the house of Judah shall walk with the house of Israel, and they shall come together out of the land of the North to the land that I have given for an inheritance unto your fathers." Jer. 3:18. This language portrays, not the return of a subservient remnant, after the 70 years captivity, but the return of a sovereign people to "possess their possessions", as Obadiah words it. We have already considered this prophecy. It was not fulfilled by the return of a few Jews, to live in subjection to the Medes and the Romans, and, latterly, the Turks. It is in process of fulfilment now—in these days and at this time. I will humour my critic so far as to say that these are LIVE ISSUES OF THIS DAY. We know that Judah is now beginning to take possession: but who is with him? The BRITISH. Oh! The Bible says it would be the HOUSE OF ISRAEL. Then let the Bible stand or fall by British-Israel truth.

CHAPTER XXIII.

We have noted the broad aspect of the commission of Jeremiah; now we shall try to sketch in brief outline some of the actual happenings of his time. It is extremely difficult to condense a story drawn from these wonderful Bible passages, every one of which is a temptation to discourse at length. The best I can hope to do in these pages is to pick out the bare thread of events, and try to marshal the facts, leaving the reader to verify them by study of the chapters.

The dealings of Jeremiah with the kings of Judah extended from the reign of the good King Josiah to the overthrow of Zedekiah in the 11th year of his reign. Zedekiah was the last king to reign over the Jewish nation. Our interest mainly centres on the last king, and the events from his time forward. To Zedekiah, the prophet was commanded to declare the impending destruction of Jerusalem by Nebuchadnezzar, and the taking into captivity of the House of Judah. Associated with the prophet is Baruch the scribe, who was evidently his assistant or secretary. As might be surmised, the prophet's mission was decidedly unpopular. His enemies "devised devices" against him; the "priests and the prophets" and "all the people" seized him at different times, saying "thou shalt surely die". And he **would** surely have died had there ever been a unanimous vote on the matter; but somehow he always seemed to have a friend—raised up, pro tem, and for the occasion. At one time it was Ahikam the son of Shaphan, "whose hand was with Jeremiah". At another time "the princes" took his part against "the prophets"; while again it was "the princes" who said unto the King. "We beseech thee let this man be put to death";

He had been in a dungeon but was taken out by the king's order and kept "in the court of the prison". Yet, once more, the king was readily persuaded to hand him over to his enemies, who let him down with ropes into a loathsome pit, where he sank in the mire and was left to die; only to be rescued again by command of the king at the request of an Ethiopian eunuch. And so the king and the princes and the prophets and "all the people" passed their 'white elephant' back and forth to each other: at their wit's end, they did not know what to do with him, but they were plainly afraid of him. From the whole account we see that the enemies of Jeremiah were mere pawns in the hands of God. The prophet was under Divine protection, preserved as we surely may conclude in order to carry out his unique mission—the latter part of it—I mean the "building and planting". Another "servant of God", Nebuchadnezzar, king of Babylon, might be trusted to perform the actual physical uprooting which Jeremiah proclaimed; but the building and planting would have to be personally conduct-by by Jeremiah himself.

We are bound to believe that the "building and planting" part of this mandate was of importance certainly as vital as the uprooting, yet strange to say it is utterly ignored by orthodox theology, or spiritualized into vague non-existence. They tell us, on absolutely no authority, Biblical or historical, that it was the planting of Christ's Kingdom, or "in other words, the Church" that was foretold here. I agree that it was Christ's Kingdom, an earthly kingdom, to merge in some way into the heavenly at His return. I have no theories to advance as to how that merger is to come about, or when. Students of the great Pyramid measurements believe that they can set the date very approximately. I am not a student of the Pyramid, and so I am sticking to my text. Christ said the Kingdom was to be given to another nation, not to a church. Certainly no church can lay claim to having been planted by Jeremiah. Yet God sanctified and ordained Jeremiah as the planter of that which was to be planted. Does the ordination of any Bishop of the Church take precedence to the ordination of Jeremiah by Jehovah ? As theologians the churchmen are altogether too superficial: as spiritual counsellors they strangely miss. the spirit of faith. They believe in the Bible account of the literal uprooting of the throne of David, simply because it is confirmed by history, but they reject the building and planting part of the Bible record, because it is not duly set down in history. Yet they exhort us mightily to have faith. By all means; let us. Yes, the theology of the churchmen is sound—mostly.

The Church will come into her own only when she allows the word of the Lord to have free course and be glorified. Can it be gainsaid that the Lord has named a nation of people who shall glorify him ? "This people have I formed for myself, **they shall show forth my praise**". Is it wrong, Reverend Sirs, to aspire that this nation may be ours ? Are we not justified in bearing witness to the proofs of our identity which no other people can produce ? No ! What does the Bible say about that ? Isaiah 43—"Let all the **nations** be gathered together .... who among them can declare this and shew us former things ? Let them bring forth their witnesses, that they may be justified; or let them hear, and say it is truth. Ye are my witnesses, saith the Lord." When other nations are unable to "shew us former things" they are exhorted to hear our witness and to **acknowledge the truth**—the truth that God has vindicated His covenant, and that there hath not failed one word of His good promise to Israel; so shall the nations be constrained to glorify the God of Jacob and seek to be taught in His ways. (See Micah 4:2).

Well, we should have no more difficulty about accepting one clause of the Divine command literally than the other:

"See I have set **thee** (Jeremiah personally) over the nations .... **to build and to plant**". Therefore, "Be not afraid of their faces, for I am with thee to deliver thee, saith the Lord." So, of course, Jeremiah did not die with his mission unfulfilled; though he certainly had a bad time. Also poor Baruch the scribe was at one time in a great state of trepidation, grief and sorrow overwhelmed him at the impending calamities to his country; he couldn't sleep nights. (Jer. 45:3). But God's message to Baruch was a command that he must brace himself to meet the inevitable. The fiat had gone forth; the doom of Judah could not be averted by mere "fainting" and "sighing"—"Thus shalt thou say unto him, The Lord saith thus: Behold, that which I have built will I break down, and that which I have planted I will pluck up, **even this whole land**." And this is followed by an assurance of personal safety similar to that given to Jeremiah his master. "Thy life will I give unto thee for a prey **in all places whither thou goest**." Indication here that Baruch was to travel far before his time came to die—not anywhere in "this whole land" was the sphere of his mission, for the whole fabric of the nation that he had been sighing about was to be "plucked up". The planting? Ah! that was to be far elsewhere, and both Baruch and Jeremiah were to take their lives "as a prey" in their hands and GO. It was a personal delegation, and personal preservation is all that was guaranteed to them. Note the significance of the warning, "Seekest thou great things for thyself? Seek them not."

Now just here I want to interject a strange passage. The people were to go into captivity: the land was to be over-run by aliens and enemies. It would be the last place in the world—for one who was aware of the impending invasion—in which to invest money in real estate. We might understand a man in Jeremiah's position naturally wanting to "cash in" on anything saleable he had; and

keeping the money for investment in the land to which he
was going. Yet we find in chapter 32 that the prophet,
who at this time was in prison, was commanded by God **to
buy a field !** Strange. And he bought it; paid seventeen
shekels of silver for it; and had all the "evidence" of the
transaction transcribed in a book and attested by witnesses.
He gave the documents into the keeping of Baruch and
charged Baruch before the witnesses, saying "Thus saith
the Lord of hosts, the God of Israel; take these evidences,
this evidence of the purchase, both which is sealed, and
this evidence which is open; and put them in an earthen
vessel, **that they may continue many days.**" You should
read the whole chapter to get the hidden meaning of this
strange transaction and note at the end of the last verse,
"For I will cause their captivity to return, saith the Lord."
This is no reference to a partial return from the Babylonian
captivity: the whole trend of this and the succeeding chapter denotes Israel and Judah both fully restored. "I will
cause the captivity of Judah, and the captivity of Israel to
return, and will build **them as at the first.**" No half measures here! And "In those days and at that time will I
cause the Branch of righteousness to grow up unto David;
and he shall execute judgment and righteousness in the
land." The "Branch of righteousness" is held by ortho-
doxy to mean Christ. One can only give an opinion on
this. If our Lord is meant here it cannot have referred to
His first coming; for we know that our Saviour held no
executive office in the land. He came to die and thereby
accomplish our redemption, for by **no other way** could
Israel have been redeemed, and brought back to covenant
mercies than by the all-sufficient atonement of our blessed
individual Saviour and national Redeemer. There is more
virtue in the Sacrifice than the orthodox Christian has been
attributing to Him. Christ has redeemed us from the curse
of the law by "dying for the nation". The law was just

but justice was satisfied by the voluntary sacrifice of our Substitute. Israel "found grace in the wilderness", hence the nation has since then been living under the regime of the Abrahamic covenant of grace. The middle wall of partition broken down, the erstwhile aliens to the commonwealth of Israel are restored to fellowship in the "covenants of promise" (Abrahamic and Davidic) Ephesians 2:12. Christ has meant all this to our race, as well as personal salvation to the individual. It is the mainspring of Anglo-Saxon progress. But from the context the "Branch of righteousness" (Not the Root or Mainspring) would appear to indicate the reigning sovereign of Israel at, or towards, the time of our Lord's second coming. "Thus saith the Lord, David shall never want a man to sit on the throne of the house of Israel." Under the Davidic covenant the throne was never to be without an occupant; but there is no assertion that the occupant should always be righteous; some of our sovereigns have not been any better than they might have been. It is "in those days" and at "that time" that the Branch of righteousness is to grow up unto David. These passages treat of the approaching climax, when Israel and Judah are to return from their captivity and be built up "as at the first," that is, under a reigning sovereign of their own, for that was their first estate. We can see the approach of that climax now. The Turks, who are the Edomites, or sons of Esau, have been ousted by the British. Obadiah told us that they were to be driven out **by Ephraim**! And the House of Jacob are even now in the act of "possessing their possessions" as they have never once done, from the days of Nebuchadnezzar until that day in December, 1917, when General Allenby walked through the Joppa gate into Jerusalem.

But what about the "evidences", so seemingly important, of that real estate deal? Our writers have usually been content with pointing out the similarity between land conveyancing as practised by the ancient Hebrews and the present day procedure under English law. But I think the real point has been overlooked. This was only a little bit of a field, yet "The Lord of Hosts", "The God of Israel", makes the "evidences" the subject of a special command ? Evidence, it seems to me, is of no use whatever **unless it can be produced**—otherwise it has no title to the name of "evidence". Well, these evidences were put in an earthen vessel, **that they might continue many days.** They were moreover, committed to the personal keeping of a faithful custodian, who, as a matter of fact, was about to leave the country never to return. Do you think he lost them—overlooked them in packing and left them behind? Hardly. Yet they have never been heard of since. There is no further reference to them in scripture as far as I know. Now, I am quite willing to be laughed at—I have given my reasons, and my conclusion is that this hidden evidence will yet be discovered; otherwise you see it would not be evidence, and the whole episode would not have been worth recording. Baruch must have taken the evidence with him and kept it all his life. It must have gone with him to the land of his destiny and in that land some day I believe it will be discovered, yet continuing in the earthen vessel even after these "many days".

CHAPTER XXIV.

When the destruction of Jerusalem drew close at hand, Jeremiah delivered a last warning to Zedekiah to give himself up to the king of Babylon, and thus submit to the righteous judgment of God. By obedience at the eleventh hour he might yet be saved; to defend the city meant to defy God, who was using Nebuchadnezzar as His instrument. Zedekiah chose the way of death, and he found it. In the 11th year of his reign the city was taken, after a siege of eighteen months. The king with some of his staff fled out of the city by night, only to be overtaken and captured on the plain of Jericho by the Chaldeans, who delivered him to the king of Babylon. "Then the king of Babylon slew the sons of Zedekiah in Riblah before his eyes: also the king of Babylon slew all the nobles of Judah. Moreover he put out Zedekiah's eyes, and bound him with chains to carry him to Babylon." This is the terrible record of the actual "rooting out" of the throne of David in Judah; and the Tribe itself was taken captive to Babylon —all except some "of the poor of the people which had nothing". These were left to till the land: and Gedaliah, son of Ahikam, one of their kindred, was appointed governor over them by the king of Babylon.

Meantime "Jeremiah abode in the court of the prison until the day that Jerusalem was taken: and he was there when Jerusalem was taken." And Nebuchadnezzar gave charge concerning Jeremiah to Nebuzaradan, the captain of the guard, saying "take him and look well to him and do him no harm; but do unto him even as he shall say unto thee." So Jeremiah, still under God's protection, was set free and given his choice of going to Babylon or remaining in Judea. He elected to remain; and joined himself to Gedaliah at Mizpah, and "dwelt among the people of the land." Gedaliah warns the people that they were to "serve," or obey the laws of the Chaldeans and the king of Babylon: for so "it might be well with them". Yet the spirit of rebellion is not stilled. Gedaliah is slain by one Ishmael, at the instigation of the king of the Ammonites.

But of what avail are all these details about a miserable remnant of "the poor of the people" left behind when the people of substance are in captivity in Babylon; the nobles and the king's sons slain, the king himself blinded and in chains in a Babylonish prison from which he never emerged? And what of the Davidic covenant—how can it be fulfilled, when we have just been told that the king's sons are slain? We see the first ray of light in chapter 41:10. After the account of the assassinations we read that Ishmael (the murderer) "carried away captive all the residue of the people that were in Mizpah, even THE KING'S DAUGHTERS and all the people .... and departed to go over to the Ammonites." This is the first mention of the king's daughters. Probably they had been left behind in Jerusalem when the king and his soldiers sallied out on to the plains of Jericho. Probably they were subsequently kept hidden for safety and so escaped notice when the rest were taken into captivity. Probably—! but really we do not know anything about it. We only read that they were at Mizpah at this time, and we accept the statement on its face value without feeling bound to explain how it came about. This is what my critic calls "naive faith". Still I feel that the onus of disproving it would be a rather heavier burden—it is beyond the memory of man! The time was 588 years before the Christian era; and we have at least the record of the Jewish historian of the time on our side; while our critics have—nothing! Just that.

Before Ishmael could join the Ammonites with his captives they were rescued by Johanan, who now became leader. He and all his captains then sought Jeremiah to tell them what was the will of the Lord. Jeremiah tells them God's will is that they should abide in the land. But their fit of meekness is soon over. They say, "It is peaceful in Egypt, there we shall see no war, and there will we dwell". And Jeremiah warns them that those who go to Egypt **to sojourn there** shall be overtaken by the sword which they feared and the famine whereof they were afraid; none were to escape. We see.—chapter 42:22, —that this sweeping judgment is pronounced against all who should be found in the place (Egypt) **whither you desire to go and to sojourn.** It will be noticed here that a loophole is left for some who might go to Egypt against their will. But the warning is discarded: "Azariah and Johanan and all the proud men" answer Jeremiah saying: "Thou speakest falsely; the Lord our God hath not sent thee to say, Go not into Egypt to sojourn there. But **Baruch, the son of Neriah, setteth thee on against us."** We see that Baruch, the faithful scribe, is still with Jeremiah.

So Johanan took them all to Egypt (Jer. 43:6). "Even men, women and children, AND THE KING'S DAUGH-TERS, and every person .... and Jeremiah the prophet, and Baruch the son of Neriah". This passage specifies "all the remnant of Judah", "men, women and children, and every person"; which might be considered comprehensive enough, without specializing or mentioning names, yet we are told expressly that it includes (1) the King's daughters, (2) Jeremiah, and (3) Baruch. These are the important ones ! Indication here that the fortunes of these are linked together. So they go, together, against their will into Egypt, and—disappear ! The chronicle of their movements abruptly terminates.

The latter part of the book of Jeremiah is a series of

declamations of God's judgment against the disobedient
Jews in Egypt, and against the heathen nations; beginning
with Pharaoh-necho, king of Egypt; then the Philistines,
Moab, the Ammonites, the Chaldeans, and a long list of
others. The Chaldeans had been allowed to punish Israel,
but they had overstepped their authority; they had angered
God by their atrocities, and especially by their impious
desecration of the temple: "Because ye were glad, because
ye rejoiced, O ye destroyers of mine heritage" ....
"Israel is a scattered sheep..............first the king of Assyria
hath devoured him; and last this Nebuchadnezzar, king of
Babylon, hath broken his bones." (Jer. 50:11 and 17).
"Israel" here includes the whole twelve tribes. "First", the
Northern kingdom, taken captive by the Assyrians, and,
"Last", the Southern kingdom of Judah, taken by Nebuchadnezzar. Now the Lord's vengeance is declared. The Median
revolt against Assyria took place in the first half of the 7th
century, B.C. It is believed that it was during the course
of this revolution that the Ten Tribes availed themselves
of an opportunity to make their escape across the Euphrates into Europe; which took place about the year 650
B.C. (The tradition in regard to this escape is recorded
in the Apocrypha, 2 Esdras 13:40-46). So that at Jeremiah's
time the overthrow of Assyria and the escape of the Northern captives had already been accomplished. Now comes
the turn of the king of Babylon, who is holding Judah in
durance vile. "Therefore, thus saith the Lord of hosts, the
God of Israel; I will punish the king of Babylon and his
land, as I have punished the king of Assyria." (Jer. 50:
18). And, again, "The Lord hath raised up the spirit of
the kings of the Medes: for His device is against Babylon,
to destroy it; because it is the vengeance of the Lord, the
vengeance of His temple." Here Jeremiah is looking into
the future and, after the manner of seers, telling the people
what "hath" taken place in the picture envisioned in his
prophetic gaze.

This vengeance against the desecrators of the temple was meted out in person to Belshazzar, the king of Babylon, against whom "Tekel" was pronounced; and "Peres"— for his kingdom was divided and given to the Medes and Persians. Follows then the decree of Cyrus, king of Persia, calling on such Jews as were so minded to return to Jerusalem and rebuild the temple. This return, which is the theme of the book of Ezra, marks the end of the seventy years captivity, as foretold in Jer. 29:10. According to the account in Ezra, the number of those who returned was about 50,000, all told. It is obvious that this small number could not include the Ten Tribes, as is the contention of some. But that contention is put even further beyond the bounds of possibility by the explicit statement, in Ezra 2:1, that the decree was obeyed by those "whom Nebuchadnezzar the king of Babylon had carried away unto Babylon;" hence it is clear that the Ten Tribes, having never been in Babylon, and having long previously passed over the Euphrates into Europe, were not within the jurisdiction of the decree of Cyrus. But a mere alibi is no embarrassment to the dwellers in Theological Topsy-turvydom: "Have some wine," said the Carpenter. "I don't see any wine," said Alice. "There isn't any " said the Carpenter. Indeed, up to a certain point, the position taken by my reverend critic is more logical; that is, the rejection of the Bible, lock, stock and barrel; which it appears is the only means this university scholar could think up to refute the arguments of a layman citing British-Israel facts. But there are other considerations which show that his negative theory is equally untenable. I cannot go into them at length here—surely they will occur to my readers—I would hint, for instance, at the virility of the Bible. If not supernatural, how has it lived? The Bible is the radium of literature. Its life emanates from within itself. Many organized attempts have been made to des-

troy that life—but it lives ! My critic did not explain this,
when he compared it with the annals of the Indians. As
against so crude an assertion, I would quote the trenchant
answer of our Lord to the critics of His day: "Ye do err,
not knowing the scriptures nor the power of God." Here
the power of God and the scriptures are linked. Is it any
wonder that the strictures of the critics are sterile ! But
the Bible is the vade mecum of Christianity at large; a
protracted defence of it hardly devolves on this little book.
I am writing especially for those who have some faith left,
and spirit enough to resist being dragooned up and down
such alley-ways of theology as may, from time to time, seem
good to the clerical higher critics. Their stock allusion to
the conclusions of scholars indicates a "naive" proprietor-
ship in the cult. As to that; we are from Missouri, and we
have not been shown.

Is there any finality about these "conclusions"? Not
at all. They have subjected the old writings of the Bible
to such a critical analysis and inspection as no other writings have suffered, but they have in fact arrived at no
finished "conclusion." Again, their criticism is wholly
negative and destructive, inasmuch as to see things from
their angle would necessitate sitting a few years at the feet
of some college lecturer; an interlude which, happily, is
not in the way of the general public. Yet, without a
shadow of compunction, they approach the people with a
raw proposal; as who would say, "You must unhitch your
old-fashioned faith in the Bible, and hook it up with the
findings of the professors (As we have done). It would
be impossible for us to explain to you how these findings
have been reached. (We don't quite know ourselves).
From your lack of education you could not follow the route ;
so—Take it from us."

Which brings out the fact that we must have faith in
something or other. The rest is a question of hitching

posts. No, I am not disparaging learning; what I am reflecting on is hamstrung judgment.

An American Episcopal bishop, addressing the Y.M.C.A. at Detroit in 1907, told them: "The Bible is not the Word of God, and nowhere declares itself to be such." Possibly he was technically correct, so far as, in just so many words "It nowhere declares itself to be such"? But what authority had he for his predicate, "The Bible is not the Word of God"? Is such a declaration to be found in any of the standard classics? In some book of superior authority? Or, are we just to take his word for it?

But the Professors of Exegesis sit in revolving chairs. If you hold to your old belief long enough, you may find yourself in agreement with the professors every few years, according as they come around. A little while ago they "concluded" that "St. Paul could not have written the Pastoral Epistles generally attributed to him," and preachers who wanted to be considered in the (scholarly) fashion began to announce their text as such and such a passage from "the writer of the Epistle to the Hebrews"; the question of authorship being in abeyance beyond the "conclusion" of the authorities that St. Paul was eliminated. Professor Burkett of Cambridge was reported as telling the Church Congress at Manchester in 1908 that "The old infallible Bible is taken away .... We do not now receive St. Paul as an authority upon the origin of sin and death." Note that "We" and "Now". However, it's all right again; the new Professor at Oxford, Mr. Cuthbert H. Turner, who has a great reputation for learning, we are told "Returns to the position of the scholars of yesterday, and accepts the earlier dates for certain books of the New Testament, as well as the traditional authors and destinations." (Quotation from The Christian, April 21st, 1921). And the Epistles of St. Paul "Are now recognized as his." You, I, and other small fry, who never doubted the authorship, do not count. But the chair has revolved, and St. Paul is "now" recognized—again ! Which means that those who hitch their faith to a chair, are sadly in need of post graduate courses to trim their sails according to its latest Rulings. I have dwelt on this a little, in order to disabuse anyone suffering from the obsession that a university degree constitutes a Dictatorship. After all—thank goodness—there's only one Pope.

CHAPTER XXV.

No doubt Jeremiah would have resisted being taken into Egypt, had not the King's daughters been taken, but in view of his commission we assume that he would regard the seed royal as under his special charge, and his obvious duty was to go with them as their guardian. The Bible narrative simply tells us that they were all taken to Egypt together; and Jeremiah disappears, as it were, while yet speaking. But the whole trend of our study has prepared us to expect nothing else than a disappearance. Since the Tribe of Dan was already established in Ireland, under the cognomen of "Tuatha da Danaan", and were at this time the only settled representatives of the House of Israel in the world, to Ireland must the prophet go, incognito, in order to fulfill his mission TO BUILD AND TO PLANT the throne of David in the House of Israel. To go openly would have been contrary to the Divine intent, which, for the time, was to hedge up the way of Lo-ammi Israel, "that she should not find her paths." (Hosea 2:6.) Israel in their Lo-ammi state were Baal-worshippers, as we are reminded in this chapter. But the time was to come when the Lord was to be to them "Ishi" and no more "Baali."

The "Bally's" of Ireland are reminiscent of the altars of Baal; how numerous they were! Baal-poer, of the Bible has its successors in Ballyporeen and many other Bally places, whose ditches the present writer crossed many times in his rambles up and down in Ireland. All around the Kerry mountain-sides, on a Saint John's night, you might see the beacon-fires twinkling and glimmering near the horizon. Up high on Mount Brandon they would flash out,

near where the peak melts into the summer sky. I asked
a companion what all the fires were meant for; and the
answer was that they were called "Baal fires", and this
was Saint John's night.   Which did very well for an
answer, as there was a dance, and we weren't caring enough
to wonder why the Kerry peasants should be calling their
little bonfires by that queer name. If you climbed up and asked the fire-lighters, they would "inform" you that it was a
"custom" Go and ask the Blacksmith, or some other authority, and he will tell you, contemptuously, "Pishogues."
(Latin for Superstition).   So custom dies hard in Ireland, and the fire-lighters give unconscious reminiscent
evidence of the time when their antecedents, Phœnician and
Israelite together, fraternized in idolatry, "burning incense
to strange gods."

Now we are told that the God of Israel would again be
worshipped as God and not as Baal.   Lo-ammi and Lo-
ruhamah would give place to Ammi and Ruhamah—for,
"I will have mercy upon her that had not obtained mercy:
and I will say to them which were not my people, Thou art
my people; and they shall say, Thou art my God." This
blessed change was to be inaugurated through the minis-
tration of Jeremiah—but we are anticipating. The whole
book of Hosea deals mainly with Israel in contrast with
Judah.   Israel, under the simile of a Gentile woman, was
Lo-ammi and Lo-ruhamah in her banished state: while her
brethren, Ammi, and her sisters, Ruhamah, had never ceased
to worship the God of Israel, and hence, had never been
divorced. They, in fact, as everyone knows, still cling to
the tenets of Temple worship and the Law of Moses in
form. "Ephraim compasseth me about with lies, and the
house of Israel with deceit: but Judah yet ruleth with God,
and is faithful with the saints." (Hosea 11:12).   There we
have Israel and Judah contrasted.   Again, to Israel it is
said "Thy calf, O Samaria hath cast thee off .... For

from Israel was it also: the workman made it; (Jeroboam's workman) therefore it is not God: but the calf of Samaria shall be broken in pieces". (Hosea 8:5-6). The reader will, of course, bear in mind that "Samaria", the capital city, and "Ephraim", the birthright tribe, are synonyms here for the House of Israel, and do not at all refer to the House of Judah. A great deal of needless confusion arises through forgetfulness of these simple distinctions. The word Israel is sometimes used to designate the whole Twelve Tribes, and again it is sometimes applied to the Jews only, after the disappearance of the Ten Tribes; but the context will generally guide the careful student in construing the meanings of Hebrew writers of different periods, in different stages of their people's history, whose varying circumstances would have a direct bearing on the value of current terms. To forget the relativity of phraseology and circumstances leads to absurdity in any study. For instance, it must have been superficiality which led the clergyman already referred to in this book, to argue in his volume that the divorced and Lo-ammi Ten Tribes were included in Cyrus' decree or invitation to come and build the Temple, and that, without any intervening change of heart or act of repentance, and of course long prior to their Redemption ! But the Bible does not hold up to our view any such liquid interpretation of justice. The divorced ones were cast off, they could not be brought back until the act of Redemption, by the death of their Substitute, had intervened. That is the story we read in the Bible, Old Testament and New.

Now let us see how it was that "Ruhamah" began to come to Israel. We are not told that Jeremiah returned from Egypt to Judea, but there is strong indication that he did return, en route, at least, for his destination: "Yet a small number that escape the sword shall return out of the land of Egypt into the land of Judah." (Jer. 44:28). Surely the prophet and his companions were amongst those who escaped the sword, for they had not gone into Egypt "to sojourn there." Did the small number return to Judea to dwell there ? No, for the kingdom had been rooted out of that "whole land," and Jeremiah must needs go to build and to plant the throne of David in the House of Israel. He would indeed find scant encouragement to settle down in Judea, under Chaldean rulers, with the temple desecrated, and all the sacred vessels considered worth while carried away to Babylon. He would likely, however, make search for some sacred thing that had been left behind by the vandals. The ark of the Covenant is not mentioned in the list of things taken to Babylon. Jeremiah would surely bring that away now if he could find it. Also the great stone, Jacob's Pillar; it had meant a lot to Israel, but it had been ignored by the Babylonians. In any case there were finer looking stones in the hanging gardens of Babylon; they would not cumber themselves with such a relic. Jeremiah, on the other hand, would bring that stone if he brought nothing else ! Now the history of the Stone of Israel would furnish a theme for a volume in itself. It has been splendidly told in Mrs. Rogers' well-known book, "The Coronation Stone," and I cannot do better than refer you to that book for a full account of it. Having made ready to depart, the little company would pass through the Land of Benjamin, for Jeremiah and Baruch were Benjamites: but they could not stay long in their homeland, for that is deserted also; none of their kindred remain; strange faces confront them everywhere. The land is desolate of friendship. Greeted with sneers and gibes, the poor wanderers move on, hurriedly, shamefacedly. "All that pass by clap their hands: they hiss and wag their head .... certainly this is the day we have looked for; we have found it, we have seen it." Lam. 2:15-16.

The picture is about the same as that of Belgium or

Northern France, during the rape. A few years ago, it was hard to believe that the things described by Jeremiah in his "Lamentations" were literally true. It is easier now. We thought the descriptions were distorted; no sort of human beings could have been capable of such bestialities. We know better now. The Bible, after all, tells the truth about human nature, and, from Nebuchadnezzar to the Kaiser, human nature, as such, has made no striking advance. These things always remind me of a remark made by a dry friend: we were discussing the "Evolution theory." He said that, while he could faintly grasp the idea of how evolution might have begun, he couldn't see why it stopped.

But harder to bear than the taunt of the stranger, is the reflection that even "The Lord was as an enemy" .... "He hath violently taken away his tabernacle .... despised in the indignation of His anger the king and the priest .... cast off His altar .... abhorred His sanctuary." Bitter indeed are the lamentations of the faithful one, to whom the sanctuary had meant so much. The Lord has abhorred His sanctuary, and the prophet's head is bowed with shame for the ruin that he could not avert. Ichabod has come to Jeremiah: are not he and his few companions the last of the hosts ! Surely the glory has departed from Israel. The throne of David is rooted out, and the homeless ones must be going.

A study of the map will show the direction they took. Egypt and the desert shut them off on the south. Moab, the Ammonites, and Babylonia, cover the East and the North. There is no choice left, for the Lord has hedged their path on three sides with enemies; only to the West is the way open. By the time they reach the coast, Jeremiah's brave heart would be regaining confidence, he would be making plans for his mission. Out there on the shore of the Mediterranean, strange to relate, there still abode some

of the coast colony of Dan, untouched by the Assyrian captivity; for, you will remember, the lot of Benjamin formed
a buffer state between them and the Assyrians, who had no
quarrel with Judah and hence would not break through
Judah's territory. So the Baal-worshipping tribe of Dan,
undisturbed, still plied their trade as merchant sailors between Palestine and their brethren in Spain, Ireland, and
Denmark. Jeremiah could readily get a vessel in which to
set sail with his precious charge; we may assume that he
would make all possible haste away from the land where
chivalry had ceased, and where licence and bestiality stalked abroad. There is no evidence that more than one of the
daughters of Zedekiah had accompanied him back from
Egypt. What became of the others is not known: subsequent tradition and history tell only of one Princess.

Now all this part of my story is pure conjecture. Nobody actually knows just how the escape was made, and
here, in common with other writers, I am drawing, more
or less, on my imagination; just as my critic said. But I
must not claim any great credit for perspicacity on that
account. It is no effort at all to "imagine" that the fugitives would break through the only port open to them.
On the other hand it would be quite a strain to imagine
that they would strive to cut their way through their
enemies, into the heart of Asia, while an easy sea-way lay
invitingly open. They couldn't go to Japan, or India, or
anywhere like that. Here we have come to what they call
the "gap." But it is not very wide, when you examine
it for yourself; it was only because you had always allowed
the critics to form your opinion for you, that you got that
wrong impression. Now we invite you to see how the gap
is bridged; more than that, we invite your suggestions, as
we are only studying the matter ourselves. Everything
is above board, so to speak, on the top of the table, and it
is plain that there is no attempt at "hoaxing", or "foist-

ing'', as has been suggested. The exact point of difference between us and our critics, is, that their contention is that the Bible prophecies are not true, and to prove this they advance some, more or less nebulous, "conclusions of scholars.'' Our contention is, that the Bible prophecies are true, and, while we base our proof on the promise itself, we point, in corroboration, to so solid a piece of circumstantial evidence as the British Empire. Meanwhile, my readers are always free to take their choice—of the contentions, and also of the proofs !

The Bible story, as we have seen, has actually left Jeremiah and his companions in such a position that the only direction they could take was West. We conclude they went West. This was about the year 588 B.C., or a little later. Question. Why do we believe they went to Ireland ? Answer—The ships of Dan would take them there; the prophecies indicate an island destination; while Irish legend and later history confirm us in the belief.

Tradition tells us that, about the year 583 B.C., a ship was wrecked on the coast of Ulster, and from it landed one who was known as the Ollam Fola, who had with him a most beautiful Eastern or Egyptian Princess, also a scribe, named Simon Bruch. They had with them a great stone, which was hailed as the "Lia Fail," or "Stone of Destiny"; also a harp. In this legend we have an explanation of the fact that the harp of David came to be the harp of Erin. The legends about these wondrous arrivals are many, and fanciful, and ornate—as all legends and folk-lore are and ought to be. Beautiful poetry in praise of the Princess was composed by the Irish bards. That is, we are assured it was beautiful, and, judging by general appearance, I am free to admit that it may have been, in its own day. But there is one thing very remarkable about these legends —I want you to notice it particularly—they were not invented by British-Israelites ! The gap, as I have said, was not very wide. There was no gap, in point of time, between the sailing of Jeremiah from Palestine, and the landing of the Ollam Fola in Ireland except what time might reasonably be allowed for the vicissitudes of the voyage, with a possible "stop-off" in Spain, for the story goes that they went first to Spain, and thereafter sailed intending to go to Denmark, only to be wrecked on the Irish coast. So the "gap" is bridged by tradition and we cross over on the bridge which we find already made. We do so, all the more cheerfully and thankfully, in that there is no gap whatever in the line of route indicated by the scriptural finger-posts..

The arrival of the travellers in Ireland was properly timed, as those who remember that things are "brought about of the Lord," may readily believe. The youthful Eochaid II. had just been elected Heremon, or "Crowned Horseman," and, so tradition says, was waiting for his coronation when the tidings of the shipwreck reached him. Ireland, then, as now, was divided into four provinces, each owning a king of its own; while, what is described by various Irish historians as a "shadowy" suzerainty, was held over the whole country by one or other of the provincial kings, who was elevated by election: for although at no time in its history was Ireland a united nation, yet there was, in those ancient times of the pre-Christian era, and down to the time of Brian Boru, a chimerical union for the ostensible purpose of mutual defence. Nor can the Sinn Fein Irish truthfully point to this as a time of united nationhood, for the historians tell us that the chief relations between the "shadowy" overlord and the provincial kings, was an effort on his part to collect tribute, and, on their's, to resist paying it. There was war in Ireland in those days.

CHAPTER XXVI.

At various junctures in the course of Jeremiah's career, we are told "the word of the Lord came to him", inspiring him how he was to act. Now there is no reason to suppose that the Divine guidance was ever withdrawn; and, basing our belief on these precedents, we may reasonably conclude that, after the shipwreck, the word of the Lord came once again to Jeremiah, to tell him that this Ireland was the island home of Israel, in which God had chosen to plant the throne of David. There is no doubt whatever, in any case, that Jeremiah acted boldly and with full assurance that he had reached his destination. He immediately set about arranging the marriage that was to consummate his life-mission. This end was happily accelerated by the love conceived by the young King for the maiden, whom those generous legends depict as the most beautiful Princess upon whom the sun had ever shone! and no less by her love for him, for had he not just been chosen as Chief by his peers, and was he not the most gallant Prince in all the land!! So, at headquarters, Jeremiah's task was easy. Nevertheless there were conditions which the good Ollam must, and did, impose. Chief of these was the stipulation, that idolatry must cease. The King, for himself, must renounce Baal-worship, and thereafter, institute such reforms as would banish it from his realm. This he consented to do, the more readily, as the priests of Baal were making themselves a nuisance by their fanatical impositions.

So it came to pass that the King of Uliad, or Ulster, was converted to the worship of the God of Israel, and united in marriage with Tea Tephi, daughter of Zedekiah, the last King of Judah, who in her person brought the line of David to reign over the House of Israel: for we believe that

by this union was fulfilled the Word of God in Ezekiel 17:-
22-23. "Thus saith the Lord God; I will also take of the
highest branch of the high cedar, and will set it; I will crop
off from the top of his young twigs a tender one, and will
plant it upon an high mountain and eminent: In the mountain of the height of Israel will I plant it: and it shall bring
forth boughs, and bear fruit, and be a goodly cedar: and
under it shall dwell all fowl of every wing; in the shadows
of the branches thereof shall they dwell.   And all the trees
of the field shall know that I the Lord have brought down
the high tree and exalted the low tree, have dried up the
green tree, and have made the dry tree to flourish: I the
Lord have spoken it and have done it."   This passage is,
of course, replete with metaphor.   "Trees" represent
nations.   "Fowls of the air of every wing," are people of
all races.   "The mountain of the height of Israel"—"an
high mountain and eminent," would be the centre of that
wide-spread Kingdom of Israel, under whose flag all manner
of races should dwell. (A condition which the world as we
know it has never seen, outside of the British Empire.)
The high tree, and the low; the green tree, and the dry, I
take to designate the Houses of Judah and Israel, respect-
ively.   Law-abiding Judah, the high and the green; divorced and banished Israel, the low and the dry.   Their
positions were to be reversed; the high was to be brought
down, and the low exalted.   Or it may, as some think,
have reference to the Pharez and Zarah lines, in the same
order.   In any case, the one supposition involves the other.
The high cedar would be the kingly line of David.   The
"tender one" cropped off from the top of his young twigs,
would be the daughter of Zedekiah; our own Princess; for
whose far away memory we feel the promptings of loyalty
and affection.   Was it not in her person that the "breach"
in the Pharez line was healed, and by her union with the
descendant of Zarah, the "Seed", she became the ancest-

ress of the present English Royal Family! She is the connecting link through whom that ancient line has descended unbroken, even as it was sworn unto King David. The following may suffice as showing the line of descent:—

From David to Zedekiah—18 kings of the House of Judah.

Tea Tephi, daughter of Zedekiah, married Eochaid II, about the year 583 B.C.

From Eochaid II. and Tea Tephi, 54 generations of the royal line of Ulster bring us to Fergus Mor MacEarca, who invaded Scotland, A.D. 503, gave to the South-west of Scotland the name of Dalriada, the same as that of the kingly seat in Ulster, and established the line of the kings of Argyleshire.

From Fergus, 13 generations of the kings of Argyle descend to Alpin; whose son, Kenneth MacAlpin, was the first king of all Scotland.

From Kenneth MacAlpin to King James VI.—26 generations in the Scottish line.

From James VI. of Scotland, and I. of England, 11 generations bring us to our gracious Soverign King George V., of Great Britain and Ireland and the British Dominions beyond the seas; under the ægis of whose sceptre, if one may so adapt the metaphor, dwell indeed "fowl of every wing," people of all races; in whose Empire alone is the Bible prophecy vindicated.

(I wish to say that, in presenting the foregoing information, I have endeavored to reduce the mass of names to readable proportions. I have at hand, in the books of three different authors, the full lists of the names, from which I take my count of the number of generations in each of the foregoing lines of kings, and believe the count to be substantially correct, but, as I have no competence as a genealogist, I wish to make this reservation clear. All information on this subject, I believe, has its source in the late Mr. Glover's well attested researches. His genealogical chart was authentic enough to have been presented to, and graciously accepted and kept by the late Queen Victoria.)

A comprehensive discussion of the Irish legends would occupy more space than this book can afford. It would also impose what would be for me an impossible condition, that is, study of the ancient annals at first hand. Indeed very few writers have found themselves at leisure to do this. To the personal researches of the late Rev. F. R. A. Glover, M.A., sometime Chaplain of the British Consulate at Cologne, we are indebted for much of our detail in this particular sphere of the subject, and this gentleman's work has been amply corroborated by a few able scholars, who have happily been able to devote their time to the study. I have made a habit, in this work, of quoting the Bible as my authority. Let the foregoing remarks indicate my authority for such excursions as I must make, away from the Biblical records.

The Psaltar of Tara was a book of chronicles of the Irish kingdom, instituted at Tara by the Ollam Fola. "Ollam Fola" is a name of Hebrew origin. Mr. Glover quotes a letter from a Jewish friend, which gives a very significant translation of the word "Olam", viz.:—"If the word was spoken as relating to a man, it would simply imply that he was the possessor of hidden knowledge, which was not common to men generally." Well might such a name belong to Jeremiah! The word "Fola" comes from the Hebrew "Fla", meaning "Wonderful". So we have Jeremiah's appropriate title as "Ollam Fola", or, in English "Wonderful Seer." Now these researches have included study of the "Annals of the Four Masters"; Lynch's "Cambrensis Eversus"; the "Annals of Clonmacnoise"; and many other scripts of ancient authority on matters, the which those who have never examined their sources, speak of airily and slightingly as myths and fables; not reflecting that these ancient chronicles must have had their origin in fact, for the Hebrew and Irish affinities, of name and annal, could not, by hook and by crook, have been mere coincidences a hundred times repeated.

In order to bring about the desired reforms, Jeremiah, or the Ollam Fola, as we now know him, founded at Tara "A fair palace for the learned sort of the realm." This was named Mer-Almin, or Mur-Ollamhan—House of the Wise Men, or School of the Prophets As we have it in these degenerate days a "University." Pity it is that some of our university men think so disrespectfully of the first ancestor of their respective Alma Maters. This same Mur-Ollamhan was the original college from whence irradiated that learning, which at length attracted students from all parts of the continent of Europe Those were the glorious days of Ireland, when she, and not pagan Rome, was the source of learning and the centre of civilization in the western hemisphere. Poor Ireland ! By what foul imposture has she been betrayed ? Then and now O tempora ! O mores !

Jeremiah, himself, was the Ard Ollam, or High Prophet, of the School of the Prophets. It is hardly to be doubted that Baruch exercised his office as Scribe in being the actual chronicler of the annals, which have been preserved as the history of those brave days of old. The name of the Princess "Tea Tephi" is not Celtic, but Hebrew "Tephi, in Hebrew, implies everything combined in mind, person, and nature, that is delectable and admirable in woman." (Glover). She died young, and her husband erected over her tomb, as a monument of his love and his sorrow, the great mound, now known as the Hill of Tara.

"Tephi was her name, she excelled all virgins!
  Wretched for him who had to entomb her
Sixty feet of correct admeasurement
  Were marked as a sepulchre to enshrine her."
            (Translation from an ancient Irish Poem).

The word "Tara" is Hebrew for the Law. The tomb over which the mound was erected was called the Mergech, which, in Hebrew again, means a resting place or depository. The legends are, that, as well as Tea Tephi's remains, the great Mergech contains the Ark of the Covenant, which was the receptacle of the stone tables of the Law. "But," the objector may say, "Would not Jeremiah have restored the Law, as the code for his new converts? Why bury the Ark of the Covenant?" In which case the objector must be reminded that the Israelites in Ireland, though converted to the true worship, were still, in their relation to the Law, uncovenanted; looking towards their Redemption, not by the letter of the Law, whose outraged majesty now demanded that it be laid aside. "In those days, saith the Lord, they shall say no more: The ark of the covenant of the Lord: neither shall it come to mind: neither shall they remember it: neither shall they visit it; neither shall that be done any more." Men had failed to achieve the righteousness of the Law; that test may not be applied again. They were taught to hope for the New Covenant.

The Lia Fail, or Stone of Destiny, upon which Eochaid and Tea Tephi were crowned, continued to be used for that purpose by all the Irish kings, until Fergus, son of Earc, took it to Scotland. Thereafter it was used by the kings of Argyleshire and of Scotland, being at one period enshrined in an abbey church at Scone, whence for a while it was known as the Stone of Scone. Thence it was taken to England by Edward I., after his victories in Scotland, and deposited in Westminster Abbey, where it lies to this day, enclosed in the Coronation Chair, upon which every British Sovereign is crowned. Thus this Stone of Destiny, claimed by tradition to be that upon which Jacob rested his head when God appeared to him in a vision at Luz, which he renamed "Bethel," has an authentic Irish, Scottish, and English history, covering a period of 2500 years.

It has taken these three countries within the scope of its itinerary, in mute evidence that their destiny is linked and welded for all time. Vain will be the present efforts to break that union.

My story is told, but, in closing, I would add a few comments upon a phase of the subject as to which I have no more competence than any other reader of the Scriptures and observer of our times. The Destiny of our Empire! We have dwelt much upon its origin. What is its destiny? I would call attention to the 37th chapter of Ezekiel—The vision of the valley of dry bones. "Son of man, these bones are the whole house of Israel: behold, they say, Our bones are dried, and our hope is lost." .... "Behold, O my people, I will open your graves .... And shall put my spirit in you, and ye shall live, and I shall place you in your own land: then shall ye know that I the Lord have spoken it, and performed it, saith the Lord." May we not believe that this Spirit of Life, which was put into the dry bones, came by virtue of the Redeemer? Now we may look for progress! "Moreover, thou son of man, take thee one stick and write upon it, For Judah and the children of Israel his companions: then take another stick, and write upon it, for Joseph, the stick of Ephraim, and for all the house of Israel his companions: and join them one to another into one stick; and they shall become one in thy hand." I like to dream that these sticks represent flags and standards, and that they forecast a strong union, of Ephraim and Manasseh especially, for these are Joseph, Ephraim, and all the house of Israel his companions. "They shall become one in thy hand." God's League of Nations! Our subject is very much up to date after all. We are becoming quite familiar with the hope expressed by many statesmen for a closer unity of the Anglo-Saxon race. They think it is the only hope of peace for the world. Would that Ephraim and Manasseh were convinced of their unit-

ed destiny, then might foreign sown jealousies and mis-
understandings be disarmed; and though we may not look
for peace without victory, if we read our Bible aright, yet
in the assurance of this strong union of "all the house of
Israel" we shall be unafraid—"Moreover, I will make a
covenant of peace with them; it shall be an everlasting
covenant with them: and I will place them, and multiply
them, and will set my sanctuary in the midst of them for
evermore."

With this thought I shall say "a-Dieu" to my readers—
British and American—there is much more that I should
love to write, but it can wait.

ODIUM THEOLOGICUM.

Two Methodist ministers saw fit to express their views in the terms of the following letters, so that I am able to present my readers with genuine samples of the type of argument advanced against us. I would have preferred to be allowed to finish my serial, which was stopped on account of this opposition, yet there may be some advantage in examining the views of the other side :—

"Anglo-Israelism a Dangerous Delusion."

"Sir,—The following, from the scholarly pen of the late Dr. Godbey, an American scholar of high standing, will show the other side of a series of articles that have been in our paper lately on the Anglo-Israelism by a Mr. Byers.

Dr. Godbey says: "In God's Holy Bible, in Rev. 7th chap., the sealing of the Ten Tribes by the Almighty shows that all this hue and cry about the lost Ten Tribes, ransacking the world to find them and writing vast volumes, is a piece of twaddle and nonsense, making out that the Anglo Saxons are identified with the lost Ten Tribes, denominating Great Britain as Ephraim and America as Manasseh, is all a stratagem and hoax to flatter the English and Americans, for those nations have a superfluity of egotism and pomposity. The Anglo-Saxons are the descendants of Japheth, while the Jews are the descendants of Shem. The hypothesis which identifies the Israelites with the Anglo-Saxons is radically false."

I am sending for a copy of Dr. Barron's famous book, and shall later have more perhaps to say on this delusion. Again let me say that the secret of Great Britain's greatness is not in any relation, for there is none, to the Jew, but because Great Britain, in the 16th century, covenanted never to have any association with the man of sin, the pope, the Babylonian anti-Christ. And the Almigghty has blessed Great Britain and given her entrance into all the nations of the earth, for God has declared that those that honour Him He will honour."

The above letter was answered by the article which

comprises my 13th chapter. Whereupon my second oppon-
ent took up his parable, as follows:I

"The Anglo-Israel Theory".

"Sir,—Beginning with the issue of Aug. 10th, there has
been running in our Orange paper the romance of Anglo-
Israelism. The English or British Empire is the lost tribes
of Northern Israel. Rev. J. Puttenham, in issue of Nov.
2nd, has promised to take a shot at this edifice of cards
after he has looked up his authorities. Meanwhile a few
minor points may be discussed.

1. J. C. Walrath in the issue of Nov. 9th, referring to
Mr. Puttenham's letter, gives us a list of names of Anglo-
Israelites. I have compared this list with the contributors
to four modern Bible dictionaries, and not one of these
names appears. Undoubtedly these people named are people of estimable character, with good social standing; but
that excellence of character and social prestige do not prove
them authorities on the Bible.

2. The argument of Mr. Byers might be epitomized as
follows: God made certain promises to Northern Israel.
These have not been fulfilled as yet. They will be fulfilled.
In the situation of the British Empire and its present promise there seems, to the initiated, to be a remarkable likeness
to what was promised to Northern Israel. Hence the British
Empire is the lost ten tribes. There seem to be some wide
gaps in the whole romance. (a) Prophecy of old, as now, was
a dealing with the live issues of the day. Any predictive
element referred to the immediate future. Long-distance
prediction is an illusion of interpreters of Bible records.
Protestants will never make headway against the superstitions of the Roman Catholic Church while we cherish this
hoary sample of superstition. We will be sane when we
ever keep in mind that prophecy has not any long-distance
predictive value. This alone indicates how necessary imagination has been to Mr. Byers.

(b) Anglo-Israelites use the poetic license of literary
genius in setting aside the well-known conclusions as to the
ethnological history of the constituent elements of the British Empire. The statement that the Angles and Saxons,

etc., are not related kinsmen of German peoples may be a popular doctrine to-day, but the ultimate question is one of fact. This nemesis of fact will dog the footsteps of anyone who finds the British people, whether Saxon or Celt, of Semitic strain. Few Anglo-Saxons will feel that the glory of the British Empire is the result of and will continue because of Britain's being of Jewish or Hebrew extraction, and so heir of the promises. It might be mentioned by way of an aside that some Japanese, who live in "Isles" (so much hangs on that word !)—and whose meteoric rise to nationhood is the wonder of the day, claim their nation is the lost tribes of Israel. Will the next world war be on this claim to glory ?

(c) Mr. Byers and his fellow Anglo-Israelites come to the Bible with naive faith. God has made certain promises: the chapter and verse are given. But how has the Bible been written ? Not by a verbal statement direct from Deity. Here is where sober study of the books of the Bible destroys the illusion of those who piece verse to verse (picked out under the guidance of fad theories) and build up the scheme which they are foisting upon the Bible. The boast of patriots of old, as now, is of the greatness of their nation and of its being the favorite of Deity. One could parallel from Indian records the proud boasts of future glory which Mr. Byers quotes from the records of the Hebrews. These are not guaranteed promissory notes or certified cheques straight from heaven. The ten northern tribes when subdued by Assyria were only partly displaced. The leaders were scattered through the Assyrian empire, whose people were of the same great Semitic migration to which the Hebrews belonged. All distinction disappeared with time and intermarriage. They were lost by complete assimilation. It is an accepted conclusion of scholars that the persistence of a remnant of the exiles from Judah in Babylonia was the result of the deepening of religious insight which took place during the period between the fall of the northern kingdom and that of the southern. The northern kingdom to which Amos and Hosea preached was destroyed before the moral revival had taken deep root. These Israelites lacked the individuality which religion gave many in the sister kingdom.

It must be stated that those who smile at the imagination of Anglo-Israelites do not take any second place in their confidence in the great future before the British Empire. To-day we are seeing within the great family one member after another reaching maturity, attain self-government—see South Africa and Egypt. In this following of the star of freedom lies the reason that "the meteor flag of England shall yet terrific burn," rather than in a long-drawn and far-fetched coincidence of facts of modern English history and Bible texts about Israel."

This letter was duly signed, by a Doctor of Divinity, I am omitting the name, having no desire to interefere with his practice.

It will be noticed that his theories on prophecy leave the following points unexplained: (1) In Logic—What value might prophecy have, apart from "predictive value"? (2) In Physico-theology—How were the multitudinous seed of Abraham, nations and kings, to become "Live Issues" of his day? Or (3) In Economics—How was the uncultivated earth to support those great nations that were to burst into being in the "immediate future"? And (4) In Religion—Which part of the Christian faith is it that we are to surrender; Belief that the advent of the Messiah was foretold 4000 years before the event, or, Belief in the advent itself? And, if we are to surrender either of these fundamentals, will it make any difference if Protestants do not "make headway against the superstitions of the R. C. Church"? (Ma foi! In that case we might be lucky if we held our own; but it doesn't seem as if it would matter).

Having indulged in abstract generalities about his conception of the value of prophecy, our critic lays down his **ipse dixit,** disposing of the Ten Tribes to his own satisfaction, by a series of independent statements, which, at any rate, nobody can accuse him of "foisting on the Bible"!

Then we are asked: How has the Bible been written, and we are offered a few negative cruderies by way of answer.

My own belief, and I suppose it is shared by others, is that the Bible is a story of the Sabbath. The first four words of its text strike the key-note of the infinite—"In the beginning God." There are multitudes of people who think of the "six days" of creation as the days of a week, and I do not suppose they are going to be punished for their simplicity either. But scientists tell us that the world is very old, and with this the Bible is in full agreement. The "six days" occupied six æons of unknown ages: of how many millions of years, the archæologists would be exceedingly glad to know. But even if they could trace it back to its birth, they would still be confronted with the infinite, for—"In the beginning God."

And, Behold the creation was "very good." "And the evening and the morning were the sixth day." And God rested on the Seventh day and sanctified it. There is no mention of evening and morning of the Seventh day, because we are still living in it, and waiting for the morning. Ever since the creation of Adam has been God's Sabbath. Creation gave place to growth and nature, and man was commanded to replenish the earth. The Creator rested. Then came sin, and the holy rest was broken. So the Bible is the long story of a broken Sabbath. But the good Book holds out hopes of a restoration. We are asked how has the Bible been written. Well, it has been written in an extremely scientific manner. It is every man's book. It has simple pastures for the simple, and profound depths for the man of science.

To return to my critic. In his last paragraph, the allusion to the meteor flag is fairly nice, though it seems to put a lot of strain on the bunting. But he smiles at our imagination ! May we not, on our part, indulge in a smile at the lack of imagination, which is content with observing that many different peoples are "following the star of freedom." (Quite naturally; where else would they go!) but has no thought for the fundamental cause which made the star of freedom to rise and shine upon the meteor flag !

9 780530 551814